D1568784

$\mathcal{H}$eaven

$\mathcal{T}he$
$\mathcal{U}$ndiscovered
$\mathcal{C}$ountry

$\mathcal{R}$ON $\mathcal{R}$HODES

Resource *Publications*

An imprint of *Wipf and Stock Publishers*
199 West 8th Avenue • Eugene OR 97401

Resource *Publications*
an imprint of Wipf and Stock Publishers
199 West 8th Avenue, Suite 3
Eugene, Oregon 97401

Heaven: The Undiscovered Country
Exploring the Wonder of the Afterlife
By Rhodes, Ron
Copyright© January, 1996 Rhodes, Ron
ISBN: 1-59244-210-2
Publication date: April, 2003
Previously published by Harvest House Publishers, January, 1996 .

With fond memories,
this book is affectionately dedicated to my grandmother,
Pauline Stovall Rhodes Smith

—absent from the body but at home with the Lord
(2 Corinthians 5:8).

Acknowledgments

A SPECIAL HEARTFELT thanks to my wife Kerri and my two children, David and Kylie. How I look forward to living with them for all eternity in the heavenly country!

Thanks also to my many friends at Harvest House Publishers—Bob Hawkins, Sr., Bob Hawkins, Jr., Bill Jensen, Carolyn McCready, Steve Miller, Teresa Evenson, Janna Walkup, Julie Castle, Nadine Dockter, Sharon Burke, LaRae Weikert, Cindy Graham, Betty Fletcher, Terry Glaspey, Mary Cooper, and all the rest. It's a true pleasure working with each of you.

Contents

There is a land of pure delight,
Where saints immortal reign;
Infinite day excludes the night,
And pleasures banish pain.

(From the hymn "There is a Land of Pure Delight")

I want to know one thing:
the way to heaven—how to land safe on that happy shore.
God Himself has condescended to teach the way;
for this very end He came from heaven.
He has written it down in a book. Oh, give me that book!
At any price give me that book!
I have it—here is knowledge enough for me.
Let me be a man of one book.
Here, then, I am, far from the busy ways of men.
I sit down alone; only God is here.
In His presence I open and read His book
that I may find the way to heaven.

—*John Wesley*

"They were longing for a better country—a heavenly one. Therefore God is not ashamed to be called their God, for he has prepared a city for them."

(Hebrews 11:16)

The Undiscovered Country

In the Shakespearean play "Hamlet," death—and what lies beyond death's door—is metaphorically described as "the undiscovered country."[1] It seems an appropriate way of describing something that human beings know so very little about.

The Scriptures use the word *country* to speak of the blissful, eternal realm of heaven. Indeed, the eternal city where saints will dwell forever is described as a heavenly country (Hebrews 11:16).

We read in the pages of Holy Writ that God has "set eternity in the hearts of men" (Ecclesiastes 3:11). And from the first book in the Bible to the last, we read of great men and women of God who gave evidence that eternity permeated their hearts. We read of people like Abel, Enoch, Noah, and Abraham—each yearning to live with God in eternity.

It is of these blessed saints that Scripture reveals:

They admitted that they were aliens and strangers on earth. People who say such things show that they are looking for a country of their own. If they had been thinking of the country they had left, they would have had opportunity to return. Instead, they were longing for a better country—a heavenly one. Therefore God is not ashamed to be called their God, for he has prepared a city for them (Hebrews 11:13-16).

11

This brings to my mind the story of the unbeliever, who, seeking to comfort a dying Christian, said to him, "My poor friend, how sorry I am that you have to leave the land of the living!" But the dying man, utterly radiant, replied, "You are wrong. I am leaving the land of the dying to go to the country of the living!"[2] Here, too, was a man looking for a better country—a heavenly one.

How is it with you, my friend? Do you long for a better country, a heavenly country? In the pages that follow, we will explore what I call "the final frontier of death and the afterlife." We will explore what the Scriptures say about the eternal city where God's people shall dwell in supreme bliss forever and ever and ever.

The Brevity of Earthly Life

As we ponder the issue of heavenly life in the Holy Scriptures, one truth that stands out over and over again is the brevity of earthly life. The years pass so quickly. As I write, I am consciously aware of the sobering reality that more of my life is behind me than ahead of me. We are all aware of our mortality.

Dr. Martyn Lloyd-Jones once said, "The moment you come into this world you are beginning to go out of it."[3] His point, of course, was that the moment we are born, the inevitable process toward death begins.

Noting the brevity of life, Job, the great Old Testament servant of God, said that "man born of woman is of few days" (Job 14:1). He appealed to God, "Remember, O God, that my life is but a breath" (7:7).

The psalmist similarly pondered before God, "You have made my days a mere handbreadth; the span of my years is as nothing before you. Each man's life is but a breath"

(Psalm 39:5). Reflecting back over his life, he said, "My days vanish like smoke" (102:3).

The New Testament continues this emphasis on man's brevity. In James 4:14 we are told, "You do not even know what will happen tomorrow. What is your life? You are a mist that appears for a little while and then vanishes." First Peter 1:24 likewise instructs us that "all men are like grass, and all their glory is like the flowers of the field; the grass withers and the flowers fall."

This is a struggle we must all deal with. Life is short. The days relentlessly pass. We grow old so quickly. And then we die.

It is a sobering exercise to ponder that, should the Lord delay His coming, not only I but my beloved wife and two precious children will one day be lowered into the earth in burial. If that were the end of things, then how despondent life would be. But, praise God, we will be reunited and live forever in the heavenly country, the eternal city of God. What a glorious hope this is!

We Don't Know When We Will Die

None of us knows when we will die. The Old Testament patriarch Isaac once said, "I am now an old man and don't know the day of my death" (Genesis 27:2). We read in Ecclesiastes 9:12 that "no man knows when his hour will come: As fish are caught in a cruel net, or birds are taken in a snare, so men are trapped by evil times that fall unexpectedly upon them." In Proverbs 27:1 the wise man urged, "Do not boast about tomorrow, for you do not know what a day may bring forth." *Each new day may bring the prospect of death.*

For this reason, the wise person maintains a consistent awareness of his mortality so that he makes good use of the time God has given. The psalmist prayed, "Show me, O LORD, my life's end and the number of my days; let me know how fleeting is my life" (Psalm 39:4). Those who maintain such an awareness live with great appreciation for each new day.

Our Lives Are in God's Hands

It is natural for us to want to live as long as possible. But the actual timing of our death is in the hands of our sovereign God. He has allotted a certain time on earth for each of us. As Job said to God, "Man's days are determined; you have decreed the number of his months and have set limits he cannot exceed" (Job 14:5).

The apostle Paul in like fashion said that God "himself gives all men life and breath and everything else. From one man he made every nation of men, that they should inhabit the whole earth; and *he determined the times set for them* and the exact places where they should live" (Acts 17:25-26, emphasis added). Perhaps Paul was thinking of the words of the psalmist: "All the days ordained for me were written in your book before one of them came to be" (Psalm 139:16).

As Christians, we need not worry about the day death will occur. Our God, who loves us infinitely, is in charge of it, and we can trust Him completely. With the psalmist, we can restfully say, "My times are in your hands" (Psalm 31:15).

How We Live Matters

Scripture presents us with a bit of a paradox. Though God is portrayed as being completely sovereign over our lives and the timing of death, Scripture also indicates that *how* we live can have something to do with *how long* we live.

On the one hand, it seems clear from the Bible that people who turn from God and perpetually live in sin can actually cut short their lives. First John 5:16 makes reference to the sin that leads to death. Apparently some people in the early church lost their lives as a result of unrepentant sin (Acts 5:1-11; 1 Corinthians 5:5; 11:29-32).

On the other hand, Scripture sets forth the general principle (not a promise) that people who honor God live long lives. Proverbs 10:27 tells us, "The fear of the LORD adds length to life, but the years of the wicked are cut short" (cf. Deuteronomy 4:40; 2 Kings 20:1-6; Ephesians 6:2-3). *How we live matters!*

Redeeming the Time

Our knowledge of the heavenly country—the future eternal city of God—should not be an end in itself. Indeed, it should influence the way we live and how we use our time in the present.

I recently heard a speech in which a Christian leader said that the average 70-year-old man has spent a total of 24 years sleeping, 14 years working at a job, eight years engaged in various amusements, six years sitting at the dinner table, five years in transportation, four years in conversation, three years in education, and two years in studying and reading. His other four years were spent in miscellaneous pursuits—except for the hour he spent every Sunday at church, as well as about five minutes per weekday engaged in prayer. This amounts to a comparatively humble total of five months that the average 70-year-old man gives to God over his life span. *Five months!*

A man by the name of Theodore W. Brennan once wrote a poem entitled, "Those Wasted Years." In it, he portrays the

tragedy of a man who spent the majority of his life apart
from a relationship with Christ:

> I looked upon a farm one day,
> That once I used to own;
> The barn had fallen to the ground,
> The fields were overgrown.
>
> The house in which my children grew,
> Where we had lived for years—
> I turned to see it broken down,
> And brushed aside the tears.
>
> I looked upon my soul one day,
> To find it too had grown,
> With thorns and nettles everywhere,
> The seeds neglect had sown.
>
> The years had passed while I had cared
> for things of lesser worth;
> The things of Heaven I let go
> When minding things of Earth.
>
> To Christ I turned with bitter tears,
> And cried, "O Lord, forgive!
> I haven't much time left for Thee,
> Not many years to live."
>
> The wasted years forever gone,
> The days I can't recall;
> If I could live those days again,
> I'd make Him Lord of all.[4]

It is with this kind of sobering reflection in mind that
theologian David C. Needham once commented, "Out of all
the eternal ages of our existence as God's children, these tiny
years here on earth have a destiny that can never be

repeated. The Bible tells us that in the stench of a sick and rotting world we are perfume bottles for the fragrance of Christ (2 Corinthians 2:15). In the gathering darkness we shine as stars (Philippians 2:15). If only we could grasp the awesome implications of these few years!"[5]

How about it? When you are 70 years old, will hindsight be kind or cruel to you?

As you read about the undiscovered country in this book, may each page motivate you to wholly and unreservedly commit yourself to living for Christ, the divine architect of the eternal city (John 14:1-3). Live daily for Him. Serve Him with joy. Walk with Him in fellowship. Make Him the center of your life. You will find that to walk daily with Christ is to daily experience a little foretaste of heaven.

Angels, joyful to attend,
Hov'ring, round thy pillow bend;
Wait to catch the signal giv'n,
And escort thee quick to heav'n.
Saints in glory perfect made,
Wait thy passage through the shade;
Ardent for thy coming o'er,
See, they throng the blissful shore.

—Augustus M. Toplady (1740-1778)[1]

1

Entering Death's Door

THE STORY IS told of the famed philosopher Diogenes looking intently at a large collection of human bones piled one upon another. Alexander the Great stood nearby and became curious about what Diogenes was doing. When he inquired, the reply was, "I am searching for the bones of your father, but I cannot seem to distinguish them from those of the slaves." Alexander got the point. *All are equal in death.*

Death has been called the great equalizer. It afflicts the young and the old, the weak and the strong, the king and the commoner, the rich and the poor, the educated and the ignorant, both male and female, and people of all colors. Death has no favorites. All are equally victims of the grim reaper. In this world of uncertainty, you can count on death. From the moment of birth, human beings are on their steady way toward death.

Current estimates are that at least 50 million people die every year throughout the world. At any one time, approximately one million people are in the process of dying in the United States alone.[2] With the aging of America—with a larger and larger percentage of the American public entering old age—the issue of death has understandably become extremely relevant.

Prior to the early twentieth century, most Americans died at about age 50 due to illness, and death normally occurred in the home. Typically the dying person's family would gather in the home, often at the person's bedside, and the person was helped to prepare for impending death.

By the middle of the twentieth century, however, death in America had become a more private matter. People didn't want to discuss it anymore. Even though death is a universal experience, people did not want to think about it until absolutely compelled to.

In their attempt to avoid dealing with the issue head-on, people would often discuss matters related to death and dying in disguised terms and with clever euphemisms. Instead of saying someone *died*, people would say he or she "passed away" and was "laid to rest." Instead of making reference to the *grave* or the *cemetery*, people would speak of "perpetual family plots."

In their feeble attempt to defeat the grim reaper, some people have even paid so-called experts in the "science of cryonics" to take their freshly dead bodies, drain the blood, fill the body with freezer fluid, encase it in aluminum, and suspend it in a bath of liquid nitrogen. Far in the future, when a cure has been discovered for whatever disease caused that person's death, it is hoped that the body can be thawed and cured, and the person can resume living.[3] *Such folly!*

In recent years, beginning in the 1980s, Americans have become much more open to talking about death. It is no longer a taboo subject. Perhaps largely because of the aging of America, it has become a topic of great relevance and people want to know more about it.

A 1994 report tells us that "nearly 80 million baby boomers—one-third of the U.S. population—have reached an age in which they are confronting mortality, through the passing of a parent, the loss of a sibling or friend, or pains beneath their own breastbones." The report goes on to note: "Spurred by this mass experience, as well as by medical advances that enable doctors to prolong dying—if not living— the once-verboten subject of death has become a national topic of conversation."[4]

What Happens at the Moment of Death?

Modern science tells us that death involves the "cessation of all life (metabolic) processes."[5] But seen in such terms, death is strictly a physical, material event. It does not give recognition to the nonmaterial (spiritual) part of man.

This brings to mind a preacher in England who once said, "I remember talking to a medical student who just that morning had dissected his first human corpse. The body had been there in front of him on the bench and he had cut away different parts of the anatomy. It was like a lifeless wax model. He said to me, shaken a little from his first experience, 'If this is all that we become at death, what is the point of anything?' "[6]

From a biblical perspective, human beings are made up of both a material part (the physical body) and an immaterial part (the soul or spirit). When a human being physically dies, his or her immaterial part departs from the material body.

The New Testament Greek word for *death* literally means "separation." At the moment of death, man's spirit or soul separates or departs from his body. This is why, when Stephen was being put to death by stoning, he prayed, "Lord Jesus, receive my spirit" (Acts 7:59). Verses such as this indicate that death for the believer involves his or her spirit departing from the physical body and immediately going into the presence of the Lord in heaven. Death for the believer is thus an event that leads to a supremely blissful existence.

For the unbeliever, however, death holds grim prospects. Indeed, at death the immaterial part (soul or spirit) departs from the material body and goes not to heaven but to a place of horrific suffering (Luke 16:19-31).

After death, both believers and unbelievers remain in a disembodied state until the future day of resurrection. And for believers, what a glorious day that will be! God will reunite believers' spirits with their resurrected physical bodies. These bodies will be specially suited to dwelling in heaven in the direct presence of God—the perishable will be made imperishable and the mortal will be made immortal (1 Corinthians 15:53). Unbelievers, too, will be resurrected, but they will spend eternity apart from God. (We'll talk more about these matters later in the book.)

The Sin-Death Connection

In Scripture we see a direct connection between sin and death (Romans 5:12). One causes the other. Death came into the universe because of sin.

This means that death is not natural. It is an unnatural intruder. God intended for human beings *to live*. Death is therefore foreign and hostile to human life. Death has arisen because of our rebellion against God; it is a form of God's judgment.

But there is grace even in death. For death, as a judgment against sin, serves to prevent us from living forever in a state of sin. When Adam and Eve sinned in the Garden of Eden (Genesis 2:17; 3:11), God assigned an angel to guard the Tree of Life. This was to protect against Adam and Eve eating from the Tree of Life while they were yet in a body of sin. How horrible it would be to live eternally in such a state!

By death, then, God saw to it that man's existence in a state of sin had definite limits. And by sending a Savior into the world—the Lord Jesus Christ—God made provision for taking care of the sin problem (John 4:42). Those who believe in Him will live eternally at His side.

Man's Natural Fear of Death

Job fittingly referred to death as the king of terrors (Job 18:14). The psalmist likewise said, "My heart is in anguish within me; the terrors of death assail me" (Psalm 55:4). Hebrews 2:15 indicates that the fear of death on the part of Old Testament saints made them subject to bondage all their lifetime. They were virtually enslaved by the fear of death.

Death is a great enemy of *all* human beings. Death strikes down the good and the wicked, the strong and the weak. Without any respect of persons, death carries its campaign of rampage and destruction through whole communities and nations.

There is something in each of us that shrinks back from the very mention of death. After all, God created us to live. *Life is natural.* But when sin entered the world, the universe was invaded by death. *Death is unnatural,* as noted earlier. Even the apostle Paul—a spiritual giant if there ever was one—considered death the "last enemy" to be conquered (1 Corinthians 15:26).

Except for those Christians who will be instantly trans-
formed into a state of glory at the future rapture,* all
Christians will eventually go through death's door. There will
come a time when our spirits will depart from the body.

As Paul said, however, death no longer has the sting it once
had before we became Christians (1 Corinthians 15:54-57).
Because of what Christ accomplished at the cross, and His
subsequent resurrection from the dead, we need never be
distracted by death's ever-present threat again. Because He is
risen, we too shall rise!

I recall the story of a boy and his father who were traveling
in a car when a bee flew through the open window. The boy
was so highly allergic to bee stings that both he and his father knew that his life was in danger. As the boy frantically
jumped around and tried to avoid the agitated bee, the father
calmly reached out and grabbed it. When he opened his
hand, the bee began to fly again, terrorizing the boy once
more. The father then said, "Look, son," holding up a hand
with an implanted stinger, "his stinger is gone; he can't hurt
you any longer." As a bee loses its stinger when it stings, so
also death lost its sting for the Christian when it stung Jesus
on the cross.

The great Bible expositor Donald Grey Barnhouse once
told a story related to the Christian and the prospect of
death. He had just attended the funeral of his wife. His
young child was with him. After leaving the funeral, they
stopped at a light where a large truck sped by, its shadow
engulfing them for a brief moment.

---

*The rapture is that event immediately prior to the beginning of the tribulation
period, when believers will be physically snatched off the earth by Christ. At that
time believers will receive their glorified resurrection bodies. *See* 1 Thessalonians
4:13-17.

Turning to his child, Barnhouse asked, "Tell me, would you rather have been hit by the truck or its shadow?" The child responded, "Why the shadow, of course."

Barnhouse reflected for a moment, and then said, "That's what happens to us Christians when we die. We are hit by the shadow of death, while those who do not know God are hit with the full force of death." Because of what Christ accomplished for us at the cross, death no longer carries the pain and horror it once did. It no longer has a stinger.

For the Christian, physical death is actually a step into life. It is not a *terminus*, but rather a *transition* into great glory. The apostle Paul once wrote, "No eye has seen, no ear has heard, no mind has conceived what God has prepared for those who love him" (1 Corinthians 2:9). Paul knew that "our present sufferings are not worth comparing with the glory that will be revealed in us" (Romans 8:18).

In view of the above, we need not fear passing through the valley of the shadow of death (Psalm 23:4). Our Lord is with us during life, and He will meet us face to face at the moment of death.

When the time comes for us to enter God's presence, He will provide us with the necessary strength and grace to make the transition without fear. I am reminded of Corrie ten Boom, who had her first experience with death after a visit to the home of a neighbor who had died. Corrie's father, seeing the worry in his daughter's eyes, said, "Corrie, when you and I go to Amsterdam, when do I give you your ticket?"

Corrie answered, "Why, just before we get on the train."

"Exactly," responded her father. "And our wise Father in heaven knows when we're going to need things too. Don't run out ahead of Him, Corrie. When the time comes that some of us will have to die, you will look into your heart and find the strength you need—just in time."

How Death Is Described in the Bible

Many people haven't the foggiest idea of what to expect beyond death's door. French philosopher François Rabelais, upon his deathbed, said, "I am going to the great Perhaps."[7]

In contrast to Rabelais, the Bible is quite clear as to what we can expect beyond death's door. Death is described in a rich variety of ways in the Bible, enabling us to understand a great deal about this mysterious event. Let's briefly probe what the Scriptures say.

The Way of All the Earth

Sometimes death is described as "the way of all the earth," emphasizing the universality of the death experience. We read, "When the time drew near for David to die, he gave a charge to Solomon his son. 'I am about to go the way of all the earth,' he said. 'So be strong, show yourself a man'" (1 Kings 2:1-2).

Joshua spoke of his death in similar fashion: "Now I am about to go the way of all the earth" (Joshua 23:14). Death is "the way of all the earth" because it is the path trodden by all human beings; no one is exempt. One day, should the Lord tarry in His coming, you and I will go "the way of all the earth." But, praise God, our spirits will be with Jesus! And one day we will be resurrected.

The Journey of No Return

Job spoke of his eventual death this way: "Only a few years will pass before I go on the journey of no return" (Job 16:22). Such words remind us of the permanence of passing from mortal life. Once we pass through death's door, we have forever left mortal life (cf. Hebrews 9:27). And this short life on earth is the only time we have to decide *for* or *against* Christ. Once we die, there is no further opportunity (or second chance) to believe in Jesus for salvation.

Being Gathered to One's People

When the Lord spoke to Moses about the impending death of Aaron, He said, "Aaron will be gathered to his people. He will not enter the land I give the Israelites. . . . Get Aaron and his son Eleazar and take them up Mount Hor. Remove Aaron's garments and put them on his son Eleazar, for Aaron will be gathered to his people; he will die there" (Numbers 20:24-26).

Death is a universal experience. Like all of his ancestors before him, Aaron died and joined all of them in death. You and I, too, will one day be gathered to *our* people—that is, Christians in heaven.

Breathing One's Last

Death is sometimes described in the Bible as breathing one's last. We read that "Ishmael lived a hundred and thirty-seven years. He breathed his last and died, and he was gathered to his people" (Genesis 25:17). Similarly, "when Jacob had finished giving instructions to his sons, he drew his feet up into the bed, breathed his last and was gathered to his people" (Genesis 49:33). Job reflected that "man dies and is laid low; he breathes his last and is no more" (Job 14:10).

This description of death focuses solely on the cessation of life in the physical body. We learn from other scriptures that once a Christian breathes his last, his spirit immediately goes into God's presence (2 Corinthians 5:8).

A Withering Away

Death is occasionally described as a withering away. Man "springs up like a flower and withers away; like a fleeting shadow, he does not endure" (Job 14:2). The flower fades. Its beauty quickly vanishes. The shadow is fleeting. It too fades. And so it is with human life.

The psalmist said to God, "You sweep men away in the sleep of death; they are like the new grass of the morning— though in the morning it springs up new, by evening it is dry and withered" (Psalm 90:5-6). Of course, this speaks only about the cessation of life in the physical body. A person's spirit certainly does not "wither away."

Departing

The great apostle Paul said, "If I am to go on living in the body, this will mean fruitful labor for me. Yet what shall I choose? I do not know! I am torn between the two: I desire to depart and be with Christ, which is better by far" (Philippians 1:22-23). Paul considered departure from earthly life and into the Lord's presence something to be desired.

When Paul knew that death was imminent, he said, "I am already being poured out like a drink offering, and the time has come for my departure" (2 Timothy 4:6). Paul was drawing on Old Testament imagery in this verse. In the Old Testament era wine was poured around the base of the altar as an offering (Numbers 15:1-12; 28:7,24). Paul viewed his own impending death—his "departure"—as an offering poured out to Christ.

Dismissal from Earthly Life

Recognizing that God alone is sovereign over the timing and circumstances of death, Simeon, after beholding the

Christ-child, said, "Sovereign Lord, as you have promised, you now dismiss your servant in peace" (Luke 2:29). In death God sovereignly dismisses a person from earthly life, at which time he or she enters the afterlife.

How does God's sovereignty over death relate to earthly causes of death? It is important to recognize that even though there may be immediate "earthly" causes of death—such as a disease, a gunshot wound, a car wreck, or the like—still, it is God who is sovereign over death.

Remember Saul in the Old Testament? First Chronicles 10:1-4 tells us that the immediate cause of Saul's death was the enemy's arrows and his own sword. But then, in verses 13 and 14, we read, "Saul died because he was unfaithful to the LORD; he did not keep the word of the LORD and even consulted a medium for guidance, and did not inquire of the LORD. So *the LORD put him to death* and turned the kingdom over to David son of Jesse" (emphasis added). Despite the immediate circumstances that brought death for Saul (arrows and a sword), God was nevertheless sovereign *behind* those circumstances.

Earthly Tent Being Destroyed

The apostle Paul graphically described death as an earthly tent being destroyed: "Now we know that if the earthly tent we live in is destroyed, we have a building from God, an eternal house in heaven, not built by human hands" (2 Corinthians 5:1).

Our present bodies, Paul said, are but temporary and flimsy abodes. They are weak, frail, and vulnerable. We "camp" in these "tents" during our journey toward heaven.

Our earthly bodies—in their present mortal state—are not designed to be lasting habitations. But a time is coming when these habitations will be resurrected, and our resurrection bodies will be permanent and indestructible. *That* is a day to look forward to.

Paradise

Jesus spoke of death in terms of entering into paradise. To one of the thieves crucified along with Him, Jesus said, "I tell you the truth, today you will be with me in paradise" (Luke 23:43).

Paradise is a place of incredible bliss and serene rest in the very presence of God (2 Corinthians 12:2-7). It is the seat and dwelling place of the divine Majesty. It is where the glorified Christ dwells. It is the residence of the holy angels. And at the moment of death, Christians enter this blessed dwelling place.

The Physical Body "Sleeps"

Death is often described in the Bible as being "asleep," for in death the body takes on the appearance of sleep. That's what Jesus was talking about when He said to the disciples, "Our friend Lazarus has fallen asleep; but I am going there to wake him up." His disciples replied, "Lord, if he sleeps, he will get better." Jesus had been speaking of death, but His disciples thought He meant natural sleep. So Jesus told them plainly, "Lazarus is dead" (John 11:11-14).

Like Lazarus, the Old Testament King David "fell asleep" in death. When David "had served God's purpose in his own generation, he fell asleep; he was buried with his fathers and his body decayed" (Acts 13:36).

Similarly, when Stephen was being stoned to death, he prayed, " 'Lord Jesus, receive my spirit.' Then he fell on his knees and cried out, 'Lord, do not hold this sin against them.' When he had said this, he fell asleep" (Acts 7:59-60).

It is critical to keep in mind that the reference to being asleep pertains *only to the physical body* and not to the soul. The soul does not sleep. It is fully conscious. The believer's soul in the afterlife is fully awake and active in the presence of God (Revelation 6:9-11). The unbeliever's soul is fully conscious in a place of great suffering (Luke 16:19-31).

The Believer's Response to Death

When Martin Luther's daughter, Magdelena, was 14 years old, she became sick and lay dying. Luther prayed, "O God, I love her so, but nevertheless, Thy will be done."

Then he turned to his daughter and said, "Magdelena, would you rather be with me, or would you rather go and be with your Father in heaven?"

The girl said, "Father, as God wills."

Luther held her in his arms as she passed away. And as they laid her to rest, he said, "Oh my dear Magdelena, you will rise and shine like the stars and the sun. How strange to be so sorrowful and yet to know that all is at peace, that all is well."

Death is still an enemy. But as we have said before, Christ has taken the sting out of death for the Christian. Luther could rest in Christ during this difficult time because he knew he would be reunited with his daughter (*see* 1 Thessalonians 4:13-16).

As we look at the lives of other great saints, we see a pattern emerge. Indeed, in each case we find them facing death not with dread but with a blessed assurance that all is well—that soon the dying one would be in the direct presence of the Lord.

- Missionary David Brainerd, on his deathbed, said, "I am going into eternity, and it is sweet for me to think of eternity."
- John Wesley, as he lay dying, said, "The best of all is, God is with us. Farewell! Farewell!"
- Susanna Wesley, on her deathbed, said, "Children, when I am gone, sing a song of praise to God."
- Lady Glenorchy, as she was dying, said, "If this is dying, it is the pleasantest thing imaginable."
- Pastor John Pawson, at the end of his life, said, "I know I am dying, but my deathbed is a bed of roses. I have no thorns planted upon my dying pillow. Heaven is already begun."[8]

Death Should Affect the Way We Live

What people believe about death tends to greatly influence how they conduct their lives. We live to a great extent in the steady consciousness that we are one day going to die. Especially as we pass middle age and head on into our senior years, we become increasingly aware that our time is winding down. What is crucial to grasp is that no matter what age we are, our understanding of death—and what lies beyond it—has everything to do with our understanding of life and its meaning.

Perhaps this is one of the most important and practical aspects of the book you are reading. Let us never forget that the Bible talks about death so that it can instruct us about life and teach us how to have an eternal perspective during our brief time on earth.

Developing an Eternal Perspective

Our true significance comes not from having attained status or accumulated earthly wealth, but from our relationship with Jesus Christ. After all, we will not take our status or earthly wealth with us into the next life. How strange, then, that so many people focus all their energies on building up that which will perish. Modern man, for the most part, has failed to maintain an eternal perspective.

Allow me to ask you a question: Do you remember the first and last names of your maternal grandmother? Most likely you do. But some people do not.

Do you remember the first and last names of your *great* grandmother? How about your *great great* grandmother? Or your *great great great* grandmother?

If you are like most people, you do not remember the names of those beyond your grandmother. And herein lies my point: As it is with your great grandmother (and beyond), *so it will one day be with you.* Just a few generations after you die, people in your own family probably will not remember your name. For all practical purposes, in their lives, it will be as though you never existed. Regardless of whether you attained high status and great wealth, you, like most other people, will not be remembered.

I say this not to depress you. I say it simply to emphasize the ultimate futility of spending all our efforts building status and wealth for this life. The things of this earth will pass. And when you enter the next life, you will leave behind all your earthly goods.

How much better it is to have an eternal perspective and recognize that our only true significance lies in our eternal relationship with Jesus Christ. Jesus spoke of this eternal perspective when He said, "Store up for yourselves treasures in heaven, where moth and rust do not destroy, and where thieves do not break in and steal" (Matthew 6:20). Such words call us to examine our lives and our priorities.

In the Presence of the Savior

As Christians, what we look forward to most following death is being in the immediate presence of the Lord. How awesome that will be! And the very knowledge that we will be with Him immediately should serve to give us strength as we face death.

There is a story of a dying man who was fearful of death, even though he was a born-again Christian. He expressed his feelings to his Christian doctor, who had made a house call. The physician was silent, not knowing what to say.

Just then a whining and scratching was heard at the door. When the doctor opened it, in bounded his big beautiful dog, who often went with him as he made house calls. The dog was glad to see his master.

Sensing an opportunity to comfort his troubled patient, the doctor said, "My dog has never been in your room before, so he didn't know what it was like in here. But he knew I was in here, and that was enough. In the same way, I'm looking forward to heaven. I don't know much about it, but I know my Savior is there. And that's all I need to know!"

> *"Weep not for me, but for yourselves."*
>
> —Words uttered by a radiant John Bunyan just before entering glory (1628-1688)[1]

2

Life in the Intermediate State

A CHILD ONCE found a bird's nest in which were some eggs. He looked upon these as a great treasure. He left them for a time. And when a week had passed, he went back again.

He returned to his mother, grieving, and said, "I had some beautiful eggs in this nest, and now they are destroyed. Nothing is left but a few pieces of broken shell."

But the mother said, "Child, here is no destruction. There were little birds within those eggs, and they have flown away, and are singing now among the branches of the trees. The eggs are not wasted, but have answered their purpose. It is far better as it is."

We can draw a lesson from this little boy's experience. When we look at our departed ones, we may be tempted to say, "Is this all you have left us, grim reaper?" But faith whispers, "No, the outer shell is broken, but the inner spirit has flown away and ascended into heaven."

Ultimately, it is not a loss for a Christian to die. It is a lasting, perpetual gain.[2] Indeed, the moment a Christian dies, his or her spirit departs from the body and goes immediately into God's presence.

This reminds me of a story evangelist Billy Graham told about his maternal grandmother. He said that when she died, the room seemed to fill with a heavenly light. "She sat up in bed and almost laughingly said, 'I see Jesus. He has His arms outstretched toward me. I see Ben [her husband who had died some years earlier] and I see the angels.' She slumped over, absent from the body but present with the Lord."[3]

Understanding the Intermediate State

Some people have wrongly assumed that immediately upon the moment of death, people receive their resurrection bodies. This is not the view of Scripture. The Bible consistently portrays the day of resurrection as yet future, and those who are presently dead do not yet have their resurrection bodies. They await the future resurrection in great anticipation.

The state of our existence between physical death and the future resurrection is properly called "the intermediate state." It is an *in-between* state—that is, it is the state of our existence in between the time our mortal bodies die and the time we receive our resurrection bodies in the future.

The intermediate state, then, is a *disembodied* state. It is a state in which a person's physical body is in the grave while his or her spirit or soul is either in heaven with Christ or in a place of great suffering apart from Christ. A person's destiny in the intermediate state depends wholly upon whether he or she has placed faith in Christ during his or her earthly existence.

To help us understand this important doctrine about the intermediate state, perhaps it would be helpful to briefly review what we touched on in chapter 1. Man has both a material part and an immaterial part. Man's material part is his body, and the immaterial part is his soul or spirit (these terms are used interchangeably in Scripture). At the moment of death, man's immaterial part separates or departs from his material part. (Remember, the Greek word for death literally means "separation.")

So, at death man becomes disembodied when his or her spirit or soul departs from the physical body. That is what happened to Billy Graham's grandmother. At the moment of death, her spirit departed from her physical body and went to be with Jesus in heaven. Her body was buried in a grave a few days later.

There are many verses in Scripture that speak of the departure of the spirit at death.[4] We are told that at the moment of death "the spirit returns to God who gave it" (Ecclesiastes 12:7). At the moment of Jesus' death, He prayed to the Father, "Into your hands I commit my spirit" (Luke 23:46). When Stephen was dying while people were stoning him, he prayed, "Lord Jesus, receive my spirit" (Acts 7:59).

The Scriptures indicate that this separation of the spirit from the physical body is only a temporary situation. There is a day coming in which God will reunite each person's soul or spirit to his or her resurrection body. When that day finally arrives, human beings will never again be disembodied. They will live forever in their resurrection bodies.

Resurrected believers will live forever in the immediate presence of God. Resurrected unbelievers will spend eternity in a place of great suffering called the Lake of Fire. (We will study more about that later in the book.)

I read about a cemetery in Indiana that has a tombstone over 100 years old. This tombstone bears the following epitaph:

Pause, stranger, when you pass me by;
As you are now, so once was I.
As I am now, so you will be,
So prepare for death and follow me.

ر

An unknown passerby had read those words and scratched this reply below them:

To follow you I'm not content,
Until I know which way you went.[5]

The passerby was right. The important thing about death is *what follows* death. *Where are you going?*

Conscious Awareness in the Intermediate State

Some people have wrongly concluded that at the moment of death, consciousness vanishes. They think the soul "sleeps." That is not the view of Scripture, however. Indeed, the Bible never speaks of the soul sleeping, but only the body. That is because the body takes on the *appearance* of sleep at the moment of death.

When we examine the Scriptures, it becomes clear that man's soul or spirit is always portrayed as being fully conscious in the intermediate state. Perhaps this is nowhere better illustrated than in the story Jesus told of the rich man and Lazarus in Luke 16. Pay close attention to His words:

There was a rich man who was dressed in purple and fine linen and lived in luxury every day. At his gate was laid a beggar named Lazarus, covered with sores and longing to eat what fell from the rich man's table. Even the dogs came and licked his sores.

The time came when the beggar died and the angels carried him to Abraham's side. The rich man also died and was buried. In hell, where he was in torment, he looked up and saw Abraham far away, with Lazarus by his side. So he called to him, "Father Abraham, have pity on me and send Lazarus to dip the tip of his finger in water and cool my tongue, because I am in agony in this fire."

But Abraham replied, "Son, remember that in your lifetime you received your good things, while Lazarus received bad things, but now he is comforted here and you are in agony. And besides all this, between us and you a great chasm has been fixed, so that those who want to go from here to you cannot, nor can anyone cross over from there to us."

He answered, "Then I beg you, father, send Lazarus to my father's house, for I have five brothers. Let him warn them, so that they will not also come to this place of torment."

Abraham replied, "They have Moses and the Prophets; let them listen to them."

"No, father Abraham," he said, "but if someone from the dead goes to them, they will repent."

He said to him, "If they do not listen to Moses and the Prophets, they will not be convinced even if someone rises from the dead" (Luke 16:19-31).

It is exceedingly clear from the above passage that both believers (Christians) and unbelievers (non-Christians) are in a state of consciousness in the intermediate state, fully aware of all that is transpiring around them. It is also clear that the dead are in complete possession of their memory and even think about their loved ones who are still alive on earth.

Jesus' story indicates that no one can comfort the wicked dead (unbelievers). There is no possibility of their leaving the place of torment; and they are portrayed as being entirely responsible for not having listened in time to the warnings of

Scripture. While people are still alive on earth they are admonished, "*Now* is the day of salvation" (2 Corinthians 6:2, emphasis added). Sadly, many people fail to heed this exhortation and die before trusting in Christ.

Another passage that clearly affirms conscious existence in the intermediate state is Matthew 17:1-4. In this passage, Jesus, Peter, James, and John are on a high mountain. Jesus then became transfigured before them, and His face became as bright as the sun. At that moment, both Moses and Elijah—whose times on earth had long passed—supernaturally appeared and spoke with Jesus. Moses and Elijah appeared *from the intermediate state.** And they were fully conscious and carried on a conversation with Jesus.

So it is with all of us who die. We are fully conscious and we can converse with other people who are with us.

The Intermediate State
Prior to Christ's First Coming

Hades, in the New Testament, is portrayed as the realm of the dead.[6] Hades is the New Testament counterpart to the Old Testament *Sheol.*[7]

Many Bible scholars believe the scriptural evidence indicates that prior to the coming of Christ, people who died went to one of two compartments in Hades—either "Paradise" or "Torments." These compartments were separated by a great gulf or chasm (*see* Luke 16:19-31).[8] Since the first coming of Christ, however, believers who have died have not

---

*Moses and Elijah did not have their resurrection bodies, for the day of resurrection is still in the future. They apparently took on some form of temporary manifestation that might have been similar to the way that angels as spirit-beings can take on a temporary appearance.

gone to their designated compartment in Hades; rather, they have gone directly into God's presence in heaven (Philippians 1:21-23).

It seems that when Jesus ascended into heaven, He took believers from the "Paradise" compartment in Hades to heaven, directly into the presence of God.[9] Paradise is now said to be in heaven.

Bible scholars believe that Ephesians 4:8 may relate to this Christ-led transfer: "When he ascended on high, he led captives in his train and gave gifts to men."[10] Scholars also believe Revelation 1:18 may relate to this event, since Christ is portrayed as the One who holds "the keys of death and Hades." Christ "unlocked" Hades for the righteous dead (Christians) and took them to heaven.[11]

The Intermediate State of Christians
Since Christ's First Coming

Ever since the time of Christ, believers who have died have gone immediately into Christ's presence in heaven. One clear indication that Paradise is now in heaven is Paul's statement in 2 Corinthians 12:2 that he was "caught up" to the "third heaven," also called "paradise" (verse 4).

While in heaven Paul heard inexpressible things that he was prohibited from revealing. Apparently heaven is so incredible—so resplendently glorious—that God, for His own reasons, forbade Paul to reveal to mortals on earth what lay ahead.

With Christ in Heaven

Christians are in continuous fellowship with Christ in the intermediate state. This is evident in numerous passages. Jesus told the thief on the cross, "I tell you the truth, today you will be *with me* in paradise" (Luke 23:43, emphasis added). While being stoned to death, Stephen prayed, "Lord Jesus, receive my spirit" (Acts 7:59). The apostle Paul said, "I desire to depart and be *with Christ,* which is better by far" (Philippians 1:23, emphasis added).

It is interesting to note that the word for "depart" in Philippians 1:23 was used in Bible times in reference to a ship being loosed from its moorings to sail away from the dock. The "mooring" that kept Paul from departing to heaven was his commitment to work among believers on earth until his task was complete. His ultimate desire, however, was to "sail" directly into God's presence.[12]

The word "depart" was also used in Bible times to speak of freeing someone from chains. Here on earth, we are anchored to the hardships and heartaches of this life. In death, these chains are broken. We are set free for entry into heaven.

Along these same lines, Paul said in 2 Corinthians 5:8 that he preferred "to be away from the body and to be at home with the Lord." The Greek word for "with" in the phrase "home with the Lord" suggests very close fellowship face to face. It is a word used of intimate relationships. Paul was saying, then, that the fellowship he would have with Christ immediately following his physical death would be greatly intimate.

The world notices the joy Christians have about the glorious prospect of being with Christ at the moment of death. Around A.D. 125, a Greek by the name of Aristeides wrote a letter to one of his friends, trying to explain the extraordinary success of the new religion, Christianity. In his letter he said, "If any righteous man among the Christians passes from this world, they rejoice and offer thanks to God, and they accompany his body with songs and thanksgiving as if he were setting out from one place to another nearby."[13]

Serene Rest

Christians in the intermediate state enjoy a sense of serene rest in the presence of Christ. They have no tedious labors to attend to. All is tranquil. The apostle John said, "I heard a voice from heaven say, 'Write: Blessed are the dead who die in the Lord from now on.' 'Yes,' says the Spirit, 'they will rest from their labor . . .' " (Revelation 14:13).

This "rest" will be a *comprehensive* rest. There will be rest from all toil of the body, all laborious work, all the diseases and frailties of the body, all outward sorrows, all inward troubles, all the temptations and afflictions of Satan, and all doubts and fears. *How blessed will be that rest!*

The great preacher Charles Spurgeon told the following touching story about the restful joys of our heavenly destiny.

> I remember standing in the pulpit one sultry summer afternoon, preaching on the joys of heaven. And there was one woman's eye that especially caught my attention. I knew not why it was, but it seemed to fascinate me. And as I spoke of heaven, she seemed to drink in every word, and her eyes flashed back again the thoughts I had uttered.
>
> She seemed to lead me on to speak more and more of the streets of gold and the gates of pearl, till suddenly her eyes appeared to me to be too fixed. At last it struck me that, while I had been talking of heaven, she had gone there!
>
> I paused and asked if someone in the pew would kindly see whether the friend sitting there was not dead. And in a moment her husband said, "She is dead, sir."
>
> I had known her long as a consistent Christian. And as I stood there, I half wished that I could have changed places with her. There was not a sigh nor a tear. She seemed to drink in the thoughts of heaven, and then immediately go there and enjoy it.[14]

The Intermediate State of Nonbelievers

The intermediate state of the wicked is not a pleasant topic. But because this subject relates to our present discussion and it is addressed in the Scriptures, we must touch on it.

In brief, at the moment of death non-Christians go as disembodied spirits to a temporary place of suffering (Luke 16:19-31). There they await their future resurrection and judgment (at the "Great White Throne judgment"), with an eventual destiny in the Lake of Fire. (We will discuss the Great White Throne judgment and the Lake of Fire in detail later in this book.)

Experiencing Anguish

In Jesus' story about Lazarus and the rich man we read about what the intermediate state will be like for nonbelievers (Luke 16:19-31). The rich man—a nonbeliever—is said to be in supreme torment. He is "in agony in this fire" (verse 24). The suffering is immeasurable.

I believe the worst torment the nonbeliever will experience, however, will be the perpetual knowledge that he *could* have trusted in Christ and escaped all this. He will *always* know—throughout the endless aeons and aeons of eternity—that he *could* have enjoyed a heavenly destiny had he turned to Christ during his earthly life.

Awaiting Final Condemnation

The state of the ungodly dead in the intermediate state is described in 2 Peter 2:9: "The Lord knows how . . . to hold the unrighteous for the day of judgment, while continuing their punishment."

The word "hold" in this verse is in the present tense, which indicates that the wicked (nonbelievers) are held captive *continuously*. Peter is portraying them as condemned prisoners who are closely guarded in a jail while awaiting future sentencing and final judgment.[15]

While God holds them there, He is said to be "continuing their punishment." The word "continuing" is also in the present tense, indicating the perpetual, ongoing nature of the punishment.[16] But this punishment in the intermediate state is only temporary. As noted earlier, the wicked dead will eventually be resurrected and then judged at the Great White Throne judgment, after which time their *eternal* punishment will begin in the Lake of Fire (Revelation 20:11-15).

It is sobering to realize that Scripture represents the state of unbelievers after death as a fixed state. There is no second chance (Ecclesiastes 11:3; Luke 16:19-31; John 8:21,24; 2 Peter 2:4,9; Jude 7,13). The Scriptures also reveal that the condemnation of unbelievers is determined by actions done during mortal life (especially the action of rejecting Christ), and that no good deed(s) done during the intermediate state can alter or soften this condemnation in any way.

Once a person has passed through the doorway of death, there are no further opportunities to repent and turn to Christ for salvation (Matthew 7:22-23; 10:32-33; 25:34-46). *Woe unto those who reject Christ in this life.*

*Our Lord has written the
promise of the resurrection
not in books alone, but in
every leaf in springtime.*

—Martin Luther (1483-1546)[1]

3

Alive Forevermore: The Future Resurrection

Dr. W.B. Hinson was a firm believer in the resurrection of Christ. After a long and fruitful life of serving God, there came a time when he found himself face to face with his convictions on this crucial doctrine. He became terminally ill.

One year after the doctor gave him the diagnosis, he spoke the following words from a church pulpit: "I remember a year ago when a man in this city said, 'You have got to go to your death.' I walked out to where I live five miles out of this city, and I looked across at that mountain that I love, and I looked at the river in which I rejoice, and I looked at the stately trees that are always God's own poetry to my soul.

"Then in the evening I looked up into the great sky where God was lighting His lamps, and I said, 'I may not see you many more times, but, Mountain, I shall be alive when you are gone; and, River, I shall be alive when you cease running toward the sea; and, Stars, I shall be alive when you have fallen from your sockets in the great down-pulling of the material universe."

Dr. Hinson believed in a risen Savior. He had no doubts that his precious Christ rose from the dead 2,000 years ago. And because of this, he was able to meet his death confidently and courageously. Every time the fear of death tried to creep up on him, he merely reminded himself, *He is risen.* And the fear would vanish.

In the eternal city, where we will live forever, there is no weariness, sickness, and death. Our perfect resurrection bodies will know no limitations. Energy will never wane. There will be no further sadness nor pain. There will be only joy in the eternal presence of the Savior.

Clothed in Resurrection

God created man to be not just an immaterial being but a material-immaterial being, with both a spirit and a physical body. Hence, even though being with Christ in heaven in a disembodied state is to be preferred over this earthly life, what is even more preferable is to finally receive our resurrection bodies and live in a physical state in God's presence.

The apostle Paul alludes to this in 2 Corinthians 5:4: "While we are in this tent [our present mortal body], we groan and are burdened, because we do not wish to be unclothed but to be clothed with our heavenly dwelling, so that what is mortal may be swallowed up by life."

Paul here indicates that being "unclothed"—that is, being without a physical body—is a state of incompletion, and for him carries a sense of "nakedness." Even though departing to be with Christ in a disembodied state is "far better" (Philippians 1:23), his true yearning is to be "clothed" with a physically resurrected body (*see* 2 Corinthians 5:6-8).[2] And that yearning will be fully satisfied on that future day of resurrection.

The Resurrection of Jesus Christ

Both friends and enemies of Christianity have long recognized that the resurrection of Christ is the foundation stone of the Christian faith. The apostle Paul wrote to the Corinthians, "If Christ has not been raised, your faith is futile; you are still in your sins" (1 Corinthians 15:17).

Paul realized that every doctrine of Christianity—including that of humankind's salvation—stands or falls on the doctrine of Christ's resurrection. If Christ did not rise from the dead, then Christianity is little more than an interesting museum piece. It would therefore be well worth our while to briefly examine what the Scriptures say about this incredible event.

Following His crucifixion, Jesus' body was buried in accordance with Jewish burial customs. He was wrapped in a linen cloth. Then about 100 pounds of aromatic spices— mixed together to form a gummy substance—were applied to the wrappings of cloth around His body.

After His body was placed in a solid rock tomb, an extremely large stone was rolled against the entrance by means of levers. This stone would have weighed about two tons (4,000 pounds). Thus the stone would not have been easily moved by human beings.

Roman guards were then stationed at the tomb. These strictly disciplined men were highly motivated to succeed in all they were assigned by the Roman government. Fear of cruel punishment produced flawless attention to duty, especially during the night watches. These Roman guards would have affixed on the tomb the Roman Seal, a stamp representing Roman power and authority.

All this makes the situation at the tomb following Christ's resurrection highly significant. The Roman Seal was broken, which meant automatic crucifixion upside-down for the person who was responsible. Furthermore, the large stone was found a good distance from the entrance, as if it had been picked up and carried away. The Roman guards had also fled. The penalty in Rome for a guard leaving his assigned position was death. We can therefore assume that they must have had a substantial reason for fleeing!

The Evidence for Christ's Resurrection

Jesus first attested to His resurrection by appearing to Mary, who then told the disciples the glorious news. That evening, the disciples gathered in a room with the doors shut for fear of the Jews (John 20:19). This fear was well founded, for after Jesus had been arrested, Annas the high priest specifically asked Jesus about the disciples (18:19). Jesus had also previously warned the disciples in the upper room: "If they persecuted me, they will persecute you also" (15:20). These facts no doubt lingered in their minds after Jesus was brutally crucified.

But then their gloom turned to joy. The risen Christ appeared in their midst and said to them, "Peace be with you!" (John 20:19). This phrase was a common Hebrew greeting (*see* 1 Samuel 25:6). But on this occasion there was added significance to Jesus' words. After the way the disciples had acted on Good Friday (they all scattered like cowards after Jesus' arrest), they may well have expected a rebuke from the Lord. Instead, He displayed compassion by pronouncing peace upon them.

Jesus then showed the disciples His hands and His side (John 20:20). The risen Lord wanted them to see that it was truly He. The wounds showed that He did not have another body but the *same* body. He was dead, but now He is alive forevermore.

Over the days that followed, Jesus made many appearances and proved that He had truly resurrected from the dead. Acts 1:3 says, "He showed himself to these men and gave many convincing proofs that he was alive. He appeared to them over a period of forty days and spoke about the kingdom of God." Moreover, "He appeared to more than five hundred of the brothers at the same time, most of whom are still living, though some have fallen asleep" (1 Corinthians 15:6). It seems clear that the resurrection of Christ is perhaps the best-attested historical event of ancient times.

Weighing the Evidence

The attack on Christianity by its enemies has most often focused on the resurrection of Christ because it has been correctly seen that this event is the foundation of the Christian faith. An extraordinary attack was launched in the 1930s by a young British lawyer. He was convinced that the resurrection of Christ was sheer fantasy and fable. Perceiving that this doctrine was the keystone of the Christian faith, he decided to gather the available evidence and expose this fraud once and for all.

Since he was a lawyer, he was confident he had the necessary mental equipment to rigidly sift through all the evidence. He was determined not to admit into evidence anything that did not meet the same stiff criteria for admission that modern law courts demand.

While doing his research, however, a funny thing happened. He discovered that the case against Christ's resurrection was not nearly as airtight as he had presumed. As a result, the first chapter of the book detailing his research ended up being entitled, "The Book That Refused to Be Written." In it he describes how—after examining the indisputable evidence—he became persuaded against his will that Christ really did bodily resurrect from the dead. The book is called *Who Moved the Stone?* Its author is Frank Morison.

Morison made the same discovery that countless other people have made down through the centuries. He found that the factual evidence for Christ's resurrection is truly staggering. Canon Westcott, a brilliant scholar at Cambridge University, said it well: "Taking all the evidence together, it is not too much to say that there is no historic incident better or more variously supported than the resurrection of Christ."[3]

Sir Edward Clarke similarly said, "As a lawyer, I have made a prolonged study of the evidences for the events of the first Easter Day. To me, the evidence is conclusive, and over and over again in the High Court I have secured the verdict on evidence not nearly so compelling."[4]

Professor Thomas Arnold was the author of the famous three-volume *History of Rome* and was appointed to the Chair of Modern History at Oxford University. He was well acquainted with the value of evidence in determining historical facts. After examining all the data on Christ's resurrection, he concluded, "I know of no one fact in the history of mankind which is proved by better and fuller evidence of every sort, to the understanding of a fair inquiry, than the great sign which God has given us that Christ died and rose again from the dead."[5]

Jesus Made Possible *Our* Resurrection

What is the point of all the above? It is not just to prove that Jesus is God. It is also to set the stage for the fact that Jesus' resurrection ensures our own resurrection from the dead.

Following the death of Lazarus, Jesus told Lazarus's sister, "I am the resurrection and the life. He who believes in me will live, even though he dies; and whoever lives and believes in me will never die" (John 11:25-26). To prove His authority to make such statements, Jesus promptly raised Lazarus from the dead!

Jesus on another occasion affirmed, "This is the will of him who sent me, that I shall lose none of all that he has given me, but raise them up at the last day. For my Father's will is that everyone who looks to the Son and believes in him shall have eternal life, and I will raise him up at the last day" (John 6:39-40).

Hence, because of what Jesus Himself accomplished on our behalf, we too will be resurrected from the dead. We can rest in the quiet assurance that even though our mortal bodies may pass away in death, they will one day be gloriously raised, never again to grow old and die.

Bodies of Glory

One of the most exciting and meaningful truths about the resurrection body is that it will be a body specially suited for dwelling in the unveiled presence of God in all of His glory. This is such an interesting and important subject that I want to discuss it at length.

The Scriptures tell us that God dwells in "unapproachable light" (1 Timothy 6:16). So brilliant and glorious is this light that no mortal can survive in its midst.

There are a few occasions in Scripture during which a believer catches a brief glimpse of God's glory, and the result is always the same. The believer falls to his knees as if he is about to die.

The apostle John, for example, saw Christ in His glory and "fell at his feet as though dead" (Revelation 1:17). When Abraham beheld the Almighty, he "fell facedown" (Genesis 17:3). When Manoah and his wife saw a manifestation of the Lord, they "fell with their faces to the ground" (Judges 13:20). Ezekiel, upon seeing the glory of God, "fell facedown" (Ezekiel 3:23; 43:3; 44:4).

We often read about the glory of God and Christ in the Scriptures. The word *glory*, when used of God, refers to the luminous manifestation of God, His glorious revelation of Himself to man.[6] This definition is borne out by the many ways the word is used in Scripture. For example, *brilliant light* consistently accompanies the divine manifestation in His glory (Matthew 17:2-3; 1 Timothy 6:16; Revelation 1:16). Moreover, the word *glory* is often linked with verbs of *seeing* (Exodus 16:7; 33:18; Isaiah 40:5) and verbs of *appearing* (Exodus 16:10; Deuteronomy 5:24), both of which emphasize the visible nature of God's glory.

Moses Caught a Glimpse of God's Glory

Some time after the Exodus, humble Moses made one of the boldest requests ever made before God: "Show me your glory" (Exodus 33:18). God responded by telling Moses, "You cannot see my face, for no one may see me and live" (verse 20). But then the Lord said, "There is a place near me where you may stand on a rock. When my glory passes by, I will put you in a cleft in the rock and cover you with my hand until I have passed by. Then I will remove my hand and you will see my back; but my face must not be seen" (verses 21-23).

Considering that no human being can see God in His full glory and live, what Moses requested of God was more than the Lord would grant for Moses' own good. Nevertheless, God did place Moses in a cleft in a rock, apparently a cavelike crevice, and then caused His glory to pass by.

Old Testament scholar Walter Kaiser tells us that in this passage, "the glory of God refers first and foremost to the sheer weight or the reality of his presence. The presence of God would come near Moses in spatial terms."[7] But God's glory would also involve indescribable illumination that was too brilliant for a mere mortal to witness.

What, then, actually occurred during this encounter Moses had with God? Kaiser explains that

> Moses would not be able to endure the spectacular purity, luminosity, and reality of staring at the raw glory of God himself. Instead, God would protect Moses from accidental (and apparently, fatal) sight of that glory. Therefore, in a striking anthropomorphism (a description of the reality of God in terms or analogies understandable to mortals), God would protect Moses from the full effects of looking directly at the glory of God by placing his hand over Moses' face until all God's glory had passed by.[8]

It was only after God's glory had passed by Moses that God removed His gracious, protecting "hand." Then Moses would view what God permitted—that is, God's "back." But what does that mean?

We know from other Bible passages that God is Spirit and is formless (Isaiah 31:3; John 4:24). In Exodus 33:22-23, then, just as the word *hand* is an anthropomorphism, so also is the word *back* an anthropomorphism. It is significant that the Hebrew word for *back* carries the idea of *aftereffects*.[9] "Moses did not see the glory of God directly, but once it had gone past, God did allow him to view the results, the afterglow, that His presence had produced."[10]

Isaiah Caught a Glimpse of God's Glory

Moses was not the only person who encountered God's glory. While in the temple, Isaiah had a vision in which he found himself in the presence of God's glory:

> In the year that King Uzziah died, I saw the Lord seated on a throne, high and exalted, and the train of his robe filled the temple. Above him were seraphs, each with six wings: With two wings they covered their faces, with two they covered their feet, and with two they were flying. And they were calling to one another:
>
> "Holy, holy, holy is the LORD Almighty; the whole earth is full of his glory."
>
> At the sound of their voices the doorposts and thresholds shook and the temple was filled with smoke.
>
> "Woe to me!" I cried. "I am ruined! For I am a man of unclean lips, and I live among a people of unclean lips, and my eyes have seen the King, the LORD Almighty" (Isaiah 6:1-5).

This passage is rich in meaning. Isaiah 6 finds the prophet in the temple in 740 B.C., perhaps mourning the death of godly King Uzziah. He may have gone there to pray in his grief.

While in the temple, God granted Isaiah a glorious vision that would give him strength for the duration of his ministry. Isaiah saw the Lord seated on a throne, "high and exalted" (Isaiah 6:1). God's long and flowing robe points to His kingly majesty. Though an earthly king had died, the true King of the universe still reigned supreme from on high.

Isaiah saw "seraphs" above God's throne (Isaiah 6:2-3). These were magnificent angels who proclaimed God's holiness and glory. The word *seraph* comes from a root term meaning "to burn," emphasizing the purity and brightness of these angelic beings.

In God's presence, these angels covered their faces with their wings. Despite their own brightness and purity, they apparently could not look at the greater brightness and purity of God, who—as we noted earlier—dwells in "unapproachable light" (1 Timothy 6:16). Isaiah, too, found it impossible to look at the unveiled glory of God. All he could do was exclaim, "Woe to me!"

The Transfiguration of Jesus Christ

In the Transfiguration, which occurred sometime prior to Jesus' crucifixion, Jesus "pulled back the veil" of human flesh (so to speak) and allowed His intrinsic glory to shine forth in all of its splendor. While Jesus was praying, "the appearance of his face changed" (Luke 9:29). "His face shone like the sun," and His clothes also changed so that they "became as white as the light" (Matthew 17:2), or "as bright as a flash of lightning" (Luke 9:29). His clothing was "dazzling white, whiter than anyone in the world could bleach them" (Mark 9:3).

If this magnificent transformation took place at night, as Luke's account suggests (Luke 9:32,37), the scene unfolding before the disciples must have been all the more awesome, beyond the capacity of words to describe.[11] Upon hearing the Father's voice from heaven, the disciples fell facedown to the ground, terrified. But Jesus came and touched them. "Get up," he said. "Don't be afraid" (Matthew 17:7).

Jesus in His Post-Ascension Glory

Somewhere around A.D. 90—some 60 years after Jesus had risen from the dead and ascended into heaven—John had the most sweeping and panoramic vision ever received by a saint of God. This apostle was uniquely privileged to behold

Christ in His glory. John heard the glorified Lord speaking to him:

> I turned around to see the voice that was speaking to me. And when I turned I saw seven golden lampstands, and among the lampstands was someone "like a son of man," dressed in a robe reaching down to his feet and with a golden sash around his chest. His head and hair were white like wool, as white as snow, and his eyes were like blazing fire. His feet were like bronze glowing in a furnace, and his voice was like the sound of rushing waters. In his right hand he held seven stars, and out of his mouth came a sharp double-edged sword. His face was like the sun shining in all its brilliance.
>
> When I saw him, I fell at his feet as though dead. Then he placed his right hand on me and said: "Do not be afraid. I am the First and the Last. I am the Living One; I was dead, and behold I am alive for ever and ever! And I hold the keys of death and Hades" (Revelation 1:12-18).

It is no wonder that John fell before Christ as a dead man: Christ's head and hair were brilliantly white, His eyes appeared like blazing fire, and His face shone like the sun. This is not unlike the description of Jesus on the Mount of Transfiguration (Matthew 17:2), which, upon seeing, the disciples "fell facedown to the ground, terrified" (verse 6).

During Jesus' earthly ministry, John had enjoyed times of intimate fellowship with Christ and had even laid his head on Jesus' breast in the Upper Room. But now we find John falling at Christ's feet, knocked cold by His resplendent glory. John now found himself in the presence of the glorified Son of God whose power, majesty, and glory were no longer veiled as they were during Jesus' earthly ministry. John responded the only way he could: falling in helpless abandon to the ground in the presence of the Almighty.

Christians Resurrected Unto Glory

What is my point in this lengthy discussion on the incredible glory of God? My point is that in our mortality, *we simply cannot exist in the unveiled presence of God.* God lives in unapproachable light, and our bodies, as presently constituted, cannot exist in His presence.

But there is coming a day when all this will change. When we receive our glorified resurrection bodies, we will be specially suited so we can dwell in the unveiled presence of God. Just as a caterpillar has to be changed into a butterfly before he can inherit the air, so also do we need to be changed before we can inherit heaven. And once we are changed, we will be able to fellowship with Him *face to face.*

The apostle Paul tells us, "I declare to you, brothers, that flesh and blood cannot inherit the kingdom of God, nor does the perishable inherit the imperishable" (1 Corinthians 15:50). Paul affirmed that "the trumpet will sound, the dead will be raised imperishable, and we will be changed. For the perishable must clothe itself with the imperishable, and the mortal with immortality. When the perishable has been clothed with the imperishable, and the mortal with immortality, then the saying that is written will come true: 'Death has been swallowed up in victory'" (1 Corinthians 15:52-54). *What a glorious day that will be!*

Raised Imperishable, Glorious, and Powerful

In 1 Corinthians 15:42-43 the apostle Paul says of the resurrection, "The body that is sown is perishable, it is raised imperishable; it is sown in dishonor, it is raised in glory; it is sown in weakness, it is raised in power." What a forceful statement about the nature of our future resurrection bodies!

Paul here graphically illustrates the contrasts between our present earthly bodies and our future resurrection bodies. The reference to sowing ("the body that is sown") is probably a metaphorical reference to burial. Just as a person sows a seed in the ground, so also is the mortal body "sown" in the sense that it is buried in the ground.[12] What's exciting is what is "raised" out of the ground—the resurrection body.

Paul notes that our present bodies are bodies that perish. The seeds of disease and death are ever upon them. It is a constant struggle to fight off dangerous infections. We often get sick. And all of us eventually die. It is just a question of time.

Our new resurrection bodies, however, will be raised *imperishable*. All liability to disease and death will be forever gone. Never again will we have to worry about infections or passing away.

What does Paul mean when he says our present bodies are "sown in dishonor"? Any way you look at it, having your lifeless corpse lowered into a hole in the ground and having dirt heaped upon you is anything but a place of honor. We may try to bring honor to funeral services by dressing our dead loved ones in their best clothes, purchasing fancy caskets, bringing in beautiful flowers, and having people give glowing eulogies. And we *should* do all of that. But ultimately, death—despite our efforts to camouflage it—is intrinsically dishonoring. After all, man was created *to live forever* with God, not to die and be buried in the ground.

Our new bodies, by contrast, will be utterly glorious. No dishonor here. Our new bodies will never again be subject to aging, decay, or death. Never again will we be buried in the ground. How great is that truth!

Paul also notes that our present bodies are characterized by weakness. From the moment we are born, the "outer man is decaying" (2 Corinthians 4:16 NASB). Vitality decreases, illness comes, and then old age follows, with its wrinkles and decrepitude. Eventually, in old age, we may become utterly incapacitated, not able to move around and do the simplest of tasks.

By contrast, our resurrection bodies will possess great power. Never again will we tire, become weak, or become incapacitated. Words truly seem inadequate to describe the incredible differences between our present bodies (those that will be "sown" in the earth) and our future resurrection bodies.

We Will Be Raised by the Power of God Himself

Scripture consistently testifies that God will raise each of us from the dead by His own mighty power. The psalmist said, "God will redeem my life from the grave; he will surely take me to himself" (Psalm 49:15). The apostle Paul referred to God as "the God who gives life to the dead" (Romans 4:17). Paul also affirmed, "We know that the one who raised the Lord Jesus from the dead will also raise us with Jesus and present us with you in his presence" (2 Corinthians 4:14).

It is also fascinating to observe that each Person in the Trinity is involved in raising us from the dead:

- Just as the Father raised Jesus from the dead, so also will He raise us from the dead (1 Corinthians 6:14).
- Jesus is recorded as saying, "My Father's will is that everyone who looks to the Son and believes in him shall have eternal life, and *I* will raise him up at the last day" (John 6:40, emphasis added).

- Of the Holy Spirit we read, "If the Spirit of him who raised Jesus from the dead is living in you, he who raised Christ from the dead will also give life to your mortal bodies through his Spirit, who lives in you" (Romans 8:11).

Each Person in the triune God—Father, Son, and Holy Spirit—will participate in raising us from the dead!

Our Resurrection Bodies Will Be *Physical* Bodies

Scripture clearly says that our resurrection bodies will not be immaterial in nature, but rather they will be material and physical. Jesus Himself said of His resurrection body, "Look at my hands and my feet. It is I myself! Touch me and see; a ghost does not have *flesh and bones*, as you see I have" (Luke 24:39, emphasis added). Like Jesus, our resurrection bodies will have flesh and bones.

Do you remember the account of Jesus appearing to the disciples? "Though the doors were locked, Jesus came and stood among them and said, 'Peace be with you!' Then he said to Thomas, 'Put your finger here; see my hands. Reach out your hand and put it into my side. Stop doubting and believe.' Thomas said to him, 'My Lord and my God!'" (John 20:26-28). Thomas had been slow to believe, but he doubted no longer. He witnessed firsthand that Jesus had truly resurrected from the dead in a material, physical body.

What's exciting is that our bodies will be material, physical, *and* glorious—just like Jesus' resurrection body. Paul said that Christ "will transform our lowly bodies so that *they will be like his glorious body*" (Philippians 3:21, emphasis added). John said, "Dear friends, now we are children of God, and what we will be has not yet been made known. But we know that when he appears, *we shall be like him*, for we shall see him as he is" (1 John 3:2).

There is another important observation to make here: It won't be any problem for God to raise people from the dead even if they have been cremated, blown up in a war, or eaten by wild animals. As John Calvin so well put it, "Since God has all the elements at His disposal, no difficulty can prevent Him from commanding the earth, the fire, and the water to give up what they seem to have destroyed."[13]

Resurrection Will Utterly Defeat Death

Resurrection is portrayed in Scripture as that which will utterly defeat death. In Hosea 13:14 God Himself declared, "I will ransom them from the power of the grave; I will redeem them from death. Where, O death, are your plagues? Where, O grave, is your destruction?"

The apostle Paul in like manner wrote:

When the perishable has been clothed with the imperishable, and the mortal with immortality, then the saying that is written will come true: "Death has been swallowed up in victory." "Where, O death, is your victory? Where, O death, is your sting?" The sting of death is sin, and the power of sin is the law. But thanks be to God! He gives us the victory through our Lord Jesus Christ (1 Corinthians 15:54-57).

Germany's Count Bismarck once remarked, "Without the hope of eternal life, this life is not worth the effort of getting dressed in the morning."[14] Bismarck was right. Without the hope of eternal life, life is futile.

Job knew something of the brevity and futility of life. "My days are swifter than a weaver's shuttle, and they come to an end without hope" (Job 7:6). "Man born of woman is of few days and full of trouble. He springs up like a flower and withers away; like a fleeting shadow, he does not endure" (Job 14:1-2).

Yes, this life is brief and full of sorrows. And if our existence ends with the grave, what is the use? This is why the apostle Paul said, "If only for this life we have hope in Christ, we are to be pitied more than all men" (1 Corinthians 15:19). But the hope that Jesus gives goes beyond the grave, and His resurrection guarantees that our hope is founded on fact.

Paul closed by affirming that "Christ has indeed been raised from the dead, the firstfruits of those who have fallen asleep" (1 Corinthians 15:20). Christ is the firstfruits. The harvest is yet to come. All who put their trust in Him will be a part of that great harvest of individuals who will rise from the dead.

> *"If you read history, you will find that the Christians who did most for the present world were just those who thought most of the next. . . . It is because Christians have largely ceased to think of the other world that they have become so ineffective in this one."*
>
> —C.S. Lewis (1898–1963)[1]

4

Heaven: The Eternal City of God

ONE OF THE greatest evangelists to ever grace this planet, Dwight Moody, was a man who had an eternal perspective and did not fear what lay beyond death's door. He was a man who was excited about his heavenly destiny and who looked forward to living in the eternal city in the very presence of God.

The day Moody entered into glory is a day to remember. Here's the way it happened:

"Some day you will read in the papers that Dwight Moody is dead," the great evangelist exclaimed one hot Sunday in August 1899 to a New York City crowd. "Don't you believe a word of it! At that moment I shall be more alive than I am now. . . . I was born of the flesh in 1837; I was born of the Spirit in 1855. That which is born of the flesh may die. That which is born of the Spirit shall live forever."

Four months later, exhausted from years of preaching and labor, Dwight Moody was dying. Early in the morning of December 22, Moody's son Will was startled by his father's voice from the bed across the room: "Earth recedes, heaven opens before me!"

Will hurried to his father's side. "This is no dream, Will. It is beautiful. . . . If this is death, it is sweet. God is calling me and I must go. Don't call me back!"

A few hours later Moody revived to find his wife and family gathered around him. He said to his wife, "I went to the gate of heaven. Why, it is so wonderful, and I saw the children [Irene and Dwight, who had died in childhood]." Within hours the man who had stirred two nations for Christ took a few final breaths and then entered the gate of heaven.[2]

Moody's entry into glory is a perfect illustration of the fact that Christ has taken the sting out of death for the Christian (1 Corinthians 15:55). The anticipation of entering heaven is altogether sweet for people who hold Christ dear to their hearts. So, dear saint, fear not that you will die. Your Savior has you in His hands in both life *and* death.

Putting Everything Into Perspective

We have such a limited perspective on earth—this tiny little speck of a planet in a vast, seemingly endless universe. Sometimes when we go outside at night, we look up and see thousands of stars illuminating the sky. And it boggles the mind to ponder that the same Christ who created all of this is the One who is building the eternal city, our future dwelling place.

To help put everything into perspective, let us consider for a brief moment the magnitude of the stellar universe. Only about 4,000 stars are visible to the human eye without the help of a telescope. However, as creation scientist Henry M. Morris tells us, the creation's *true* vastness becomes evident when it is realized that with the giant telescopes now available, astronomers have estimated that there are about 10^{25}

stars (that is, 10 million billion billion stars) in the known universe. Scientists estimate that this is about the number of grains of sand in the world.[3]

And who but God knows how many stars exist beyond the reach of our finite telescopes? "Since God is infinite, and He is the Creator of the universe, there is no reason to assume that either our telescopes or our relativistic mathematics have penetrated to its boundaries."[4]

Not only is the grandeur of the created universe evident in the number of stars, but also in their incredible distances from each other. Theologian John MacArthur did some scientific digging and discovered the following facts about the vastness of the universe:

- The moon is only 211,453 miles away, and you could walk to it in twenty-seven years. A ray of light travels at 186,000 miles per second, so a beam of light would reach the moon in only one-and-a-half seconds.
- If we could travel at that speed, we would reach Venus in two minutes and eighteen seconds because it's only 26 million miles away.
- After four-and-one-half minutes we would have passed Mercury, which is 50 million miles away.
- We could travel to Mars in four minutes and twenty-one seconds because it's only 34 million miles away.
- The next stop would be Jupiter—367 million miles away—and it would take us thirty-five minutes.
- Saturn is twice as far as Jupiter—790 million miles—and it would take one hour and eleven seconds.
- Eventually we would pass Uranus, Neptune, and finally Pluto—2.7 billion miles away. Having gotten that far, we still haven't left our solar system. . . .

- The North Star is 400 hundred billion miles away, but that still isn't very far compared with known space.
- The star called Betelgeuse is 880 quadrillion miles from us and has a diameter of 250 million miles, which is greater than the earth's orbit. . . .
- Where did it all come from? Who made it? It can't be an accident. Someone made it, and the Bible tells us it was Jesus Christ.[5]

Is not the stellar universe indescribably amazing? And is it not astounding to realize that Christ—the One who constructed this universe (John 1:3; Colossians 1:16; Hebrews 1:2)—is the same One who is building the heavenly city in which we will dwell for all eternity (John 14:1-3)?

It is mind-stretching to ponder the fact that as glorious as the stellar universe is, it is dim in comparison to the glory of the divine abode. Indeed, as theologian Eric Sauer says, "The light in which He dwells is superior to all things visible; it is something other than the radiance of all suns and stars. It is not to be beheld by earthly eyes; it is 'unapproachable' (1 Timothy 6:16), far removed from all things this side (2 Corinthians 12:4). Only the angels in heaven can behold it (Matthew 18:10); only the spirits of the perfected in the eternal light (Matthew 5:8; 1 John 3:2; Revelation 22:4); only the pure and holy, even as He Himself is pure (1 John 3:2-3)."[6]

The eternal city is an abode of resplendent glory. God Himself dwells there. And though in our mortal bodies we cannot exist in this divine abode in the presence of God—though we cannot behold the unapproachable light with earthly eyes—our future resurrection bodies will be specially suited for living in God's presence. In the meantime, if we should die, our disembodied spirits will go directly into God's presence and enjoy His fellowship as we await that glorious resurrection day.

The Old Testament patriarch Abraham looked forward to the eternal city (Hebrews 11:10). Indeed, we are told that many Old Testament saints "were longing for a better country—a heavenly one. Therefore God is not ashamed to be called their God, for he has prepared a city for them" (Hebrews 11:16).

Christians of all ages have, like Abraham, looked forward with great anticipation to the eternal city. Presently we are but pilgrims in another land, making our way to the heavenly country. Take comfort in this realization!

The City of Glory

In Revelation 21 we find a description of the eternal city of God. This is a city of great glory, which, I believe, is what Jesus was referring to during His earthly ministry when He told the disciples: "In my Father's house are many rooms; if it were not so, I would have told you. I am going there to prepare a place for you. And if I go and prepare a place for you, I will come back and take you to be with me that you also may be where I am" (John 14:2-3). Christ Himself has prepared this glorious abode for His followers!

Presented to our amazement and awe in Revelation 21 is a scene of such transcendent splendor that the human mind can scarcely take it in. This is a scene of ecstatic joy and fellowship of sinless angels and redeemed glorified human beings. The voice of the One identified as the Alpha and the Omega, the beginning and the end, utters a climactic declaration: "Behold, I am making all things new" (Revelation 21:5 NASB).

Theologian Millard Erickson comments on the glorious splendor of this city: "Images suggesting immense size or brilliant light depict heaven as a place of unimaginable splendor, greatness, excellence, and beauty. . . . It is likely that while John's vision employs as metaphors those items which we think of as being most valuable and beautiful, the actual splendor of heaven far exceeds anything that we have yet experienced."[7] Truly, as the apostle Paul said, "No eye has seen, no ear has heard, no mind has conceived what God has prepared for those who love him" (1 Corinthians 2:9).

What is of great significance is the statement in Revelation 21:23 that "the city does not need the sun or the moon to shine on it, for the glory of God gives it light, and the Lamb is its lamp." This is consistent with the prophecy in Isaiah 60:19: "The sun will no more be your light by day, nor will the brightness of the moon shine on you, for the LORD will be your everlasting light, and your God will be your glory."

Dr. Lehman Strauss's comments on the Lamb's glory are worthy of meditation: "In that city which Christ has prepared for His own there will be no created light, simply because Christ Himself, who is the uncreated light (John 8:12), will be there. . . . The created lights of God and of men are as darkness when compared with our Blessed Lord. The light He defuses throughout eternity is the unclouded, undimmed glory of His own Holy presence. In consequence of the fullness of that light, there shall be no night."[8]

The Three "Heavens" of Scripture

The Scriptures make reference to the "third heaven"—which is the ineffable and glorious dwelling place of God (2 Corinthians 12:2). It is elsewhere called the "heaven of heavens" and the "highest heaven" (1 Kings 8:27; 2 Chronicles 2:6).

If God's abode is called the third heaven, then what are the first and second heavens? Scripture gives us the answer. The first heaven is the earth's atmosphere (Job 35:5). The second heaven is the stellar universe (Genesis 1:17; Deuteronomy 17:3).

Now, here is why this is significant: In Revelation 21:1 we read, "Then I saw a new heaven and a new earth, for the first heaven and the first earth had passed away, and there was no longer any sea." *Which heaven (or heavens) will pass away and be made new?*

The only heavens that have been negatively affected by man's fall are the first and second heavens—earth's atmosphere and the stellar universe. The entire physical universe is running down and decaying. But the third heaven—God's perfect and unstained dwelling place—remains untouched by man's sin. It needs no renewal. It is already perfect. This heaven subsists in moral and physical perfection, and undergoes no change.[9]

Hence, when Scripture talks about the passing away of the old heaven and earth, and introduces a new heaven and earth, the "heaven" referred to is not God's dwelling place but rather the first and second heavens. And when these heavens along with the earth are made new, there will be a much wider (all-inclusive) meaning for the third heaven. "It will embrace the new heaven, the new earth, the New Jerusalem, and indeed a sinless universe. . . . In fact, in the eternal state, the term heaven will comprehend the entire universe, exclusive of the one isolation ward for all sinners, called, Gehenna, or the lake of fire."[10] (More on this in the next chapter.)

Descriptions of Heaven in Scripture

We have already touched upon heaven as the "eternal city." But the Bible also describes heaven in other ways. And each description reveals something new and exciting about heaven. Let's briefly examine some of these.

The Heavenly Country

Hebrews 11 is the Faith Hall of Fame in the Bible. In this pivotal chapter we read of the eternal perspective of many of the great faith warriors in biblical times:

> All these people were still living by faith when they died. They did not receive the things promised; they only saw them and welcomed them from a distance. And they admitted that they were aliens and strangers on earth. People who say such things show that they are looking for a country of their own. If they had been thinking of the country they had left, they would have had opportunity to return. Instead, they were longing for a better country—a heavenly one (Hebrews 11:13-15).

This passage tells us that the great warriors of the faith were not satisfied with earthly things. They looked forward to "a better country." And what a glorious country it is. Eighteenth-century Bible expositor John Gill contemplates how the heavenly country

> is full of light and glory; having the delightful breezes of divine love, and the comfortable gales of the blessed Spirit; here is no heat of persecution, nor coldness, nor chills of affection; here is plenty of most delicious fruits, no hunger nor thirst; and here are riches, which are solid, satisfying, durable, safe and sure: many are the liberties and privileges here enjoyed; here is a freedom from a body subject to diseases and death, from a body of sin and death, from Satan's temptations, from all doubts, fears, and unbelief, and from all sorrows and afflictions.[11] Selah!*

---

*"Selah" is an ancient Hebrew term often used by the psalmist, which is loosely translated, "Pause and think about that."

The Holy City

In Revelation 21:1-2 we find heaven described as the holy city. This is a fitting description. Indeed, in this city there will be no sin or unrighteousness of any kind. Only the pure of heart will dwell there.

This doesn't mean you and I must personally attain moral perfection before we can live there. Those of us who believe in Christ have been given the very righteousness of Christ. Because of what Christ accomplished for us at the cross (taking our sins upon Himself), we have been made holy (Hebrews 10:14). Hence, we will have the privilege of living for all eternity in the holy city.

The Home of Righteousness

Second Peter 3:13 tells us that "in keeping with his promise we are looking forward to a new heaven and a new earth, *the home of righteousness*" (emphasis added).

What a perfect environment heaven will be to live in! During our earthly lives, we have to lock up our houses and we fear the possibility of intruders breaking in. There is so much *un*righteousness. But heaven will be the home of righteousness. It will therefore be a perfect environment to live in for those who have been made righteous by Christ.

The Kingdom of Light

Colossians 1:12 refers to heaven as "the kingdom of light." Christ, of course, is the light of the world (John 8:12). The eternal *kingdom* thus takes on the character of the *King*. Christ, "the light of the world," rules over "the kingdom of light." Moreover, it is Christ's own divine light that illumines the holy city of light (Revelation 21:23). How glorious it will be!

The Paradise of God

The word *paradise* literally means "garden of pleasure" or "garden of delight." Revelation 2:7 calls heaven "the paradise of God." In 2 Corinthians 12:4 the apostle Paul said he "was caught up to paradise" and "heard inexpressible things, things that man is not permitted to tell."

Apparently this paradise of God is so resplendently glorious, so ineffable, so wondrous, that Paul was forbidden to say anything about it to people still in the earthly realm. But what Paul saw instilled in him an eternal perspective that enabled him to face the trials that lay ahead of him.

The New Jerusalem

Perhaps the most elaborate biblical description of the heavenly city is found in Revelation 21, where we read about the New Jerusalem. This city measures approximately 1,500 miles by 1,500 miles by 1,500 miles. It is so huge that it would measure approximately the distance between the Mississippi River and the Atlantic Ocean.

The eternal city could either be cube-shaped or pyramid-shaped. It may be preferable to consider it shaped as a pyramid, for this would explain how the river of the water of life can flow down its sides as pictured in Revelation 22:1-2.

As we read John's description of the New Jerusalem, we find a whole series of contrasts with the earth, which Bruce Shelley summarizes for us:

In contrast to the darkness of most ancient cities, John says heaven is always lighted. In contrast to rampant disease in the ancient world, he says heaven has trees whose leaves heal all sorts of sicknesses. In contrast to the parched deserts of the Near East, he pictures heaven with an endless river of crystal-clear water. In contrast to a meager existence in an arid climate, John says twelve kinds of fruit grow on the trees of heaven. In a word, heaven is a wonderful destiny, free of the shortages and discomforts of this life.[12]

Revelation 21:12 tells us that the New Jerusalem has "a great, high wall with twelve gates, and with twelve angels at the gates. On the gates were written the names of the twelve tribes of Israel." Moreover, we are told, "the wall of the city had twelve foundations, and on them were the names of the twelve apostles of the Lamb" (Revelation 21:14).

Perhaps the angels are at each of the twelve gates not only as guardians but also because of their role as ministering spirits to the heirs of salvation (Hebrews 1:14). Perhaps the names of the twelve tribes of Israel are written on the gates to remind us that "salvation is of the Jews" (John 4:22 KJV). And perhaps the names of the apostles appear on the foundations to remind us that the church was built upon these men of God (Ephesians 2:20).

The "river of the water of life" has intrigued Bible interpreters since the first century. In Revelation 22:1 we read, "The angel showed me the river of the water of life, as clear as crystal, flowing from the throne of God and of the Lamb down the middle of the great street of the city."

Perhaps one of the best explanations is that this pure river of life, though it may be a real and material river, is symbolic of the abundance of spiritual life that will characterize those who are living in the eternal city.[13] The stream seems to symbolize the perpetual outflow of spiritual blessing to all the redeemed of all the ages, who are now basking in the full glow of eternal life. What spiritual blessedness there will be in the eternal state!

The Occupants of Heaven

Who dwells in heaven? This question is important, for you and I as Christians will spend all eternity with the other occupants of heaven.

God

First and foremost, heaven is where God Himself dwells. Heaven is God's natural habitat. We read in Psalm 102:19 that the Lord looks down "from his sanctuary on high," and "from heaven" He views the earth. We are told, "The LORD has established his throne in heaven, and his kingdom rules over all" (Psalm 103:19). The Lord Himself says, "Heaven is my throne, and the earth is my footstool" (Acts 7:49).

The Angels

Though angels apparently have access to the entire universe, it appears from the testimony of Scripture that angels actually live in heaven but are sent on specific errands or assignments outside of heaven (*see* Daniel 9:21; cf. Mark 13:32).[14] There are many passages in Scripture that speak of heaven—and not earth—as the primary home of angels. For example:

- Micaiah makes mention of "the LORD sitting on his throne with all the host of heaven standing on his right and on his left" (2 Chronicles 18:18). The "host of heaven" refers to the angelic realm.

- Daniel 7:10 tells us that "thousands upon thousands" of angels attend God in heaven, and "ten thousand times ten thousand" (one-hundred million) angels stand before Him.
- Isaiah 6:1-6 pictures angels hovering around God's throne in heaven, proclaiming, "Holy, holy, holy is the LORD Almighty."
- Jesus speaks of angels "ascending and descending" to and from heaven in John 1:51.
- Hebrews 12:22 exhorts believers, "You have come to . . . the city of the living God. You have come to thousands upon thousands of angels in joyful assembly."
- John the apostle, author of the book of Revelation, said "I looked and heard the voice of many angels, numbering thousands upon thousands, and ten thousand times ten thousand. They encircled the throne and the living creatures and the elders" (Revelation 5:11).

Believers

The redeemed in heaven will be made up of people "from every tribe and language and people and nation" (Revelation 5:9). You and I—and all those who trust in Christ as Savior—will be a part of that blessed group.

For this reason, the apostle Paul confidently asserts that "our citizenship is in heaven" (Philippians 3:20). We may be earthly citizens too, but in terms of our ultimate destiny, we are truly citizens of heaven. We are pilgrims passing through, on our way to another country, another land, another city. And we behave ourselves here *below* as citizens of that city *above*.

It is fascinating to ponder that when you and I enter into glory, we will be able to perceive the angels just as clearly as you and I perceive each other here on earth (1 Corinthians

13:12). We will see them just as clearly as they see us. And we will jointly serve our glorious King—Jesus Christ—from eternity to eternity, from age to age, forevermore.

We can look forward to that day when our voices will join with the voices of the angels in worship and praise to our eternal God. This glorious scene is described in detail in the book of Revelation:

> After this I looked and there before me was a great multitude that no one could count, from every nation, tribe, people and language, standing before the throne and in front of the Lamb. They were wearing white robes and were holding palm branches in their hands. And they cried out in a loud voice: "Salvation belongs to our God, who sits on the throne, and to the Lamb." All the angels were standing around the throne and around the elders and the four living creatures. They fell down on their faces before the throne and worshiped God, saying: "Amen! Praise and glory and wisdom and thanks and honor and power and strength be to our God for ever and ever. Amen!" (Revelation 7:9-12).

"Oh, to think of heaven without Christ! . . . It is a day without the sun, existing without life, feasting without food, seeing without light. . . . It is the sea without water, the earth without its fields, the heavens without their stars. There cannot be a heaven without Christ. He is the sum total of bliss, the fountain from which heaven flows."

—Charles Spurgeon[1]

5

The Blessing of Heaven for Believers

W E'VE ALREADY SEEN that heaven holds many blessings in store for those who trust in Jesus Christ. But in what follows I would like to get a little more specific.

As we explore what the Scriptures say about the blessing of heaven for believers, keep ever before your mind what this information means *to you personally*. Heaven is not just a doctrine. Our forward gaze of heaven has everything to do with how we live as Christians in the present.

The Absence of Death

The Old Testament promises that in the heavenly state death will be swallowed up forever (Isaiah 25:8). Paul speaks of this same reality as it relates to the future resurrection: "When the perishable has been clothed with the imperishable, and the mortal with immortality, then the saying that is written will come true: 'Death has been swallowed up in victory'" (1 Corinthians 15:54). Revelation 21:4 tells us that God "will wipe every tear from their eyes.

There will be no more death or mourning or crying or pain, for the old order of things has passed away."

What an awesome blessing this is: There will be *no more death*—no more fatal accidents, no more incurable diseases, no more funeral services, no more final farewells. Death will be gone and done with, never again to be faced by those who dwell in heaven. Life in the eternal city will be painless, tearless, and deathless.

Intimate Fellowship with God and Christ

Can there be anything more sublime and more utterly satisfying for the Christian than to enjoy the sheer delight of unbroken fellowship with God, and have immediate and completely unobstructed access to the divine glory (John 14:3; 2 Corinthians 5:6-8; Philippians 1:23; 1 Thessalonians 4:17)? We shall see Him "face to face" in all His splendor and glory. We will gaze upon His countenance, and behold His resplendent beauty forever.

Surely there can be no greater joy or exhilarating thrill for the creature than to look upon the face of the divine Creator and fellowship with Him forever. He "who alone is immortal and who lives in unapproachable light" (1 Timothy 6:16) shall reside intimately among His own, and "they will be his people, and God himself will be with them" (Revelation 21:3).

In the afterlife there will no longer be intermittent fellowship with the Lord, blighted by sin and defeat. Instead, there will be continuous fellowship. Spiritual death shall never again cause human beings to lose fellowship with God, because, for believers, the sin problem will no longer be existent. When we enter into glory we will no longer have the sin nature within us. Sin will be banished from our being.

To fellowship with God is the essence of heavenly life, the fount and source of all blessing: "You will fill me with joy in your presence, with eternal pleasures at your right hand" (Psalm 16:11). We may be confident that the crowning wonder of our experience in the eternal city will be the perpetual and endless exploration of that unutterable beauty, majesty, love, holiness, power, joy, and grace which is God Himself.[2]

Revelation 21:3 assures us, "Now the dwelling of God is with men, and he will live with them. They will be his people, and God himself will be with them and be their God." God, in His infinite holiness, will dwell among redeemed human beings because Adam's curse will have been removed, Satan and the fallen angels will have been judged, the wicked will have been punished and separated from God, and the universe will have been made sinless (except for the Lake of Fire; *see* Revelation 20:15; 21:8; 22:15).

Reunion with Christian Loved Ones

One of most glorious aspects of our lives in heaven is that we will be reunited with Christian loved ones. The Christians in the church at Thessalonica were apparently very concerned about their Christian loved ones who had died. They expressed their concern to the apostle Paul. So, in 1 Thessalonians 4:13-17, Paul deals with the "dead in Christ" and assures the Thessalonian Christians that there will indeed be a reunion. And yes, believers *will* recognize their loved ones in the eternal state.

How do we know we will recognize one another? Besides the clear teaching of 1 Thessalonians 4, we are told in 2 Samuel 12:22-23 that David knew he would be reunited with his deceased son in heaven. He had no doubt about recognizing him. As well, when Moses and Elijah (who had long passed from earthly life) appeared to Jesus on the Mount of Transfiguration (Matthew 17:1-8), they were recognized by all who were present. Furthermore, in Jesus' story of the rich man and Lazarus in Luke 16:19-31, the rich man, Lazarus, *and* Abraham were all recognized by each other in the intermediate state.

Not only that, but 1 Corinthians 13:12 tells us that "now we see but a poor reflection as in a mirror; then we shall see face to face. Now I know in part; then I shall know fully, even as I am fully known." The mirrors of the ancients were made of polished metal and were far inferior to the mirrors we have today. The images were dark and indistinct. Similarly, our present knowledge is but a faint reflection of the fullness of knowledge we will have in the afterlife. This being so, we will surely recognize our Christian loved ones in the eternal state.

Related to this, many Christians have wondered whether husbands and wives will still be husbands and wives in heaven. It seems from the scriptural evidence that believers will no longer be in a married state in the afterlife. Jesus Himself said, "At the resurrection people will neither marry nor be given in marriage; they will be like the angels in heaven" (Matthew 22:30).

Of course, it will always be true that my wife Kerri and I were married on this earth. *Nothing will ever change that.* And in the eternal state, in the new heaven and the new earth, we will retain our memory that we were married on the old earth. It will be an eternal memory. And what a precious memory it will be.

We should not think of this as a deprivation. It may be very difficult for us to conceive how we could be happy and fulfilled if we were not still married to our present spouse. But God Himself has promised that not only will there *not* be any sense of deprivation, there will be only bliss, and there will be no more sorrow or pain.

My wife Kerri and I, and all other believers, are part of the glorious church, which, the Scriptures reveal, will one day be *married to Christ*. This event is referred to as the marriage of the Lamb (Revelation 19:7-9). It is an event to look forward to with great anticipation.

Still another question that comes up from time to time is whether our children will still be our children in the afterlife. *Of course they will!* It will always be true that your daughter is your daughter and your son is your son. Receiving a glorified body does not obliterate the fact that in earth-time history a husband and wife conceived and gave birth to a son or daughter.

But in the eternal state, there is also a broader relationship in which we are all equally "sons" and "daughters" in God's eternal family. We have each become adopted into His forever family (Ephesians 1:5).

Satisfaction of All Needs

In our present life on earth, there are times when people go hungry and thirsty. There are times when people's needs are not met. But in the eternal state God will abundantly meet each and every need of the redeemed.

Revelation 7:16-17 tells us, "Never again will they hunger; never again will they thirst. The sun will not beat upon them, nor any scorching heat. For the Lamb at the center of the throne will be their shepherd; he will lead them to springs of living water. And God will wipe away every tear from their eyes."

Serene Rest

The Scriptures indicate that a key feature of heavenly life is rest (Revelation 14:13). No more deadlines to work toward. No more overtime work in order to make ends meet. No more breaking our back. Just rest. *Sweet serene rest.* And our rest will be especially sweet since it is ultimately a rest in the very presence of God, who meets our every need.

Sharing in Christ's Glory

As difficult as it may be to fully understand, the Scriptures indicate that in the heavenly state believers will actually share in the glory of Christ. Romans 8:17 tells us, "If we are children, then we are heirs—heirs of God and co-heirs with Christ, if indeed we share in his sufferings in order that we may also share in his glory." Likewise, Colossians 3:4 informs us that "when Christ, who is your life, appears, then you also will appear with him in glory."

This, of course, does not mean that we become deity. But it does mean that you and I as Christians will be in a state of glory, sharing in Christ's glory, wholly because of what Christ has accomplished for us. We will have glorious resurrection bodies and be clothed with shining robes of immortality, incorruption, and splendor.

Activities of Believers in Heaven

What will we do for all eternity in heaven? Will we be sitting on clouds playing harps as some cartoons would lead us to believe?

Not by any means! There will be no purposeless inactivity in the eternal state. Scripture portrays believers as being involved in meaningful (yet restful) service throughout eternity. Let's look at just a few of the activities believers will take part in during their time in the eternal state.

Praising and Worshiping God and Christ

The book of Revelation tells us that in eternity, we will offer worship and praise before the throne of God and Christ. In Revelation 7:9-10, for example, we read of a great multitude of believers before God's throne crying out, "Salvation belongs to our God, who sits on the throne, and to the Lamb." Revelation 19:1-6 portrays a great multitude of believers shouting out hallelujahs before God's throne. This is one activity that redeemed human beings and angels will do together.

The worship that takes place in heaven will be ultimately fulfilling. As pastor Douglas Connelly points out, "Heavenly worship will not be confining or manipulated, but spontaneous and genuine. . . . We will lose ourselves in the sheer joy of expressing with our lips the adoration and love we feel for God in our hearts. . . . You won't find quiet, solemn worship clothed in hushed tones and organ music either. Instead you will hear shouts and loud voices and trumpets."[3]

Serving God and Christ

Another activity that will occupy us in the eternal state will be the perpetual serving of God and Christ. This will not be a tedious kind of service but a joyous one—fully meeting our heart's every desire.

In the opening words of the book of Revelation we read, "To him who loves us and has freed us from our sins by his blood, and has made us to be a kingdom and priests *to serve his God and Father*—to him be glory and power for ever and ever!" (Revelation 1:5-6, emphasis added; cf. 22:3). There will be no boredom in eternity. Because we will be servants of the Most High, and because there will be an endless variety of tasks to perform, the prospect of heaven is entrancingly attractive.

Based on Jesus' parable in Luke 19:11-26, it seems that faithfulness in our service to Christ during our mortal state on earth may relate to our service in the eternal state. In the parable the master affirmed to one of the servants, "Because you have been trustworthy in a very small matter, take charge of ten cities" (verse 17). If we are faithful servants in *this* life, Christ will entrust us with more in the *next* life.

It also seems that our future service will involve reigning with Christ. In Revelation 22:5 we are told that believers "will reign for ever and ever." We will be involved in some capacity in the heavenly government.

As well, part of our service will involve judging the angels. "Do you not know that we will judge angels?" Paul asks in 1 Corinthians 6:2-3. This is noteworthy because man is presently lower than the angels (*see* Psalm 8). The situation will be reversed in the eternal state. In heaven, angels will be lower than redeemed humanity.

Believers will also be serving God in the heavenly "temple." The book of Revelation tells us that believers will stand before the throne of God and *serve him day and night in his temple*" (Revelation 7:15, emphasis added). Bible expositors are careful to point out that the reference to "temple" in this verse is a metaphorical way of describing God's presence. After all, Revelation 21:22 tells us that there is no actual temple in the eternal city, for the Lord God and the Lamb are the temple. Hence, to serve God "day and night in his temple" refers to perpetually serving God in His very presence. *Glorious!*

Learning More About Our Incomparable God

Apparently we will be able to grow in knowledge in our heavenly existence. Throughout future ages believers will be shown "the incomparable riches of his grace" (Ephesians 2:7). Though our capacity for knowledge and our actual intelligence will be greatly increased, we will not be omniscient (all-knowing). Only God is omniscient. We will always maintain our capacity to learn.

This means that we will never get bored in heaven. God is so infinite—with matchless perfections that are beyond us in every way—that we will never come to the end of exploring Him and His marvelous riches.

The Old Heaven and Earth

As we think back to the scene in the Garden of Eden in which Adam and Eve sinned against God, we remember that God placed a curse upon the earth (Genesis 3:17-18). Hence, before the eternal kingdom can be made manifest, God must deal with this cursed earth. Indeed, the earth—along with the first and second heavens (the earth's atmosphere and the stellar universe)—must be renewed. The old must make room for the new.

The Scriptures often speak of the passing of the old heaven and earth. Psalm 102:26, for example, says this about the earth and the stellar universe: "They will perish, but you [O God] remain; they will all wear out like a garment. Like clothing you will change them and they will be discarded."

In Isaiah 51:6 we read, "Lift up your eyes to the heavens, look at the earth beneath; the heavens will vanish like smoke, the earth will wear out like a garment.... But my salvation will last forever, my righteousness will never fail." This reminds us of Jesus' words in Matthew 24:35: "Heaven and earth will pass away, but my words will never pass away."

Perhaps the most extended section of Scripture dealing with the passing of the old heaven and earth is 2 Peter 3:7-13:

> The present heavens and earth are reserved for fire, being kept for the day of judgment and destruction of ungodly men.... The heavens will disappear with a roar; the elements will be destroyed by fire, and the earth and everything in it will be laid bare. Since everything will be destroyed in this way, what kind of people ought you to be? You ought to live holy and godly lives as you look forward to the day of God and speed its coming. That day will bring about the destruction of the heavens by fire, and the elements will melt in the heat. But in keeping with his promise we are looking forward to a new heaven and a new earth, the home of righteousness.

The New Heaven and Earth

In Isaiah 65:17 God spoke prophetically, "Behold, I will create new heavens and a new earth. The former things will not be remembered, nor will they come to mind." In the book of Revelation we read, "Then I saw a new heaven and a new earth, for the first heaven and the first earth had passed away, and there was no longer any sea.... He who was

seated on the throne said, 'I am making everything new!' "
(Revelation 21:1,5). You and I are destined for a new heaven
and a new earth!

Bible scholars tell us that the Greek word used to designate
the newness of the cosmos is not *neos* but *kainos*. *Neos* means
new in time or origin. But *kainos* means new in nature or
quality. So the phrase "new heaven and a new earth" refers
not to a cosmos that is totally other than the present cosmos.
Rather, the new cosmos will stand in continuity with the present cosmos, but it will be *utterly renewed and renovated.*[4]

In keeping with this, Matthew 19:28 speaks of "the regeneration" (KJV). Acts 3:21 speaks of the time "for God to
restore everything." As Bible expositor Walter Scott puts it,
"Our planet will be put in the crucible, altered, changed,
and made new, to abide forever."[5]

The new earth, being a renewed and an eternal earth, will
be adapted to the vast moral and physical changes that the
eternal state necessitates. Everything will be new in the eternal state. Everything will be according to God's own glorious
nature. The new heavens and the new earth will be brought
into blessed conformity with all that God is—in a state of
fixed bliss and absolute perfection.

Commenting on the new earth, Bible scholar Edward
Thurneysen gives us these illuminating words:

> The world into which we shall enter . . . is therefore not an-
> other world; it is this world, this heaven, this earth; both,
> however, passed away and renewed. It is these forests, these
> fields, these cities, these streets, these people, that will be the
> scene of redemption. At present they are battlefields, full of
> the strife and sorrow of the not yet accomplished consum-
> mation; then they will be fields of victory, fields of harvest,
> where out of seed that was sown with tears the everlasting
> sheaves will be reaped and brought home.[6]

It seems clear that there will be geological changes in the new earth, for there will be no more sea (Revelation 21:1). At present about three-quarters of the earth's surface is covered with water and it is therefore uninhabitable. On the new earth, we will have an immensely increased land surface because of the disappearance of the oceans. Glorified humanity will inhabit a glorified earth recreated and adapted to eternal conditions.

An incredible truth to ponder is that in the next life heaven and earth will no longer be separate realms, as they are now, but will be merged. Believers will thus continue to be in heaven even while they are on the new earth.[7] The new earth will be utterly sinless, and hence bathed and suffused in the light and splendor of God, unobscured by evil of any kind or tarnished by evildoers of any description.

"Heaven" will thus encompass the new heaven and the new earth. And the New Jerusalem—the eternal city that measures 1,500 by 1,500 by 1,500 miles—will apparently "come down" and rest upon the newly renovated earth (*see* Revelation 21:2). This city, as noted earlier, will be the eternal dwelling place of the saints of all ages.

How glorious the new heaven and the new earth will be. Even on our present earth, there are parts of the world untouched by man where a person can behold the most glorious sunrise, and the scene is absolutely dazzling. And during the day the weather is virtually perfect as that person enjoys the world of nature around him. How could anyone improve on such a day?

And yet the finest earth day we can possibly experience will be as nothing, for "no eye has seen, no ear has heard, no mind has conceived what God has prepared for those who love him" (1 Corinthians 2:9).

In the golden streets of Heaven
As the happy children play,
Gentle Jesus watches o'er them,
Caring for them, day by day.
And may you find comfort, knowing
In the Father's home above
Your little one is happy
In the sweetness of His love.

— J.B. Marchbanks[1]

6

Heaven for Those Who Can't Believe

Perhaps there is nothing more difficult in the world than for a parent to bury his or her own child. How heart-wrenching it is for a mother and father to watch as the casket containing their beloved son or daughter is lowered into the ground.

Understandably, an issue of great concern to Christian parents is the eternal status of offspring who die in infancy or early childhood. Obviously infants, toddlers, and most little children do not have the capacity to "believe" in Jesus Christ. The same is true of some mentally handicapped people. They simply do not have the mental ability to place saving faith in Jesus. So what about heaven for those who can't believe? What do the Scriptures—the fountain of truth—teach?

Throughout the centuries various theories have been suggested by Christian thinkers.² Some have tried to argue that infants are sinless and morally innocent, and hence are automatically saved if they should die. But this view goes against the clear scriptural teaching that all human beings are born with a sin nature (more on this in a moment).

Others have focused their entire attention on the love of God. Since God is a God of love, it is argued, He wouldn't send an infant to hell. While this view correctly recognizes

God's love (1 John 4:8), it ignores God's other attributes—such as His holiness (1 Peter 1:16). God does not violate His holy standards in order to show love. God never "lovingly" overlooks the sin nature of any human being (including infants).

Still others have tried to argue that God by His foreknowledge looks down into the hypothetical future of the deceased child to determine whether or not he or she *would have* believed in Jesus. Those who would have believed are allegedly saved. Those who would not have believed are not saved.

All of the above viewpoints have extremely serious weaknesses from a scriptural perspective. But I do strongly believe that the Scriptures teach that every infant who dies is immediately ushered into God's glorious presence in heaven. In what follows I will present the scriptural considerations that have settled the issue in my mind.

The Universal Need of Salvation

At the outset, we must recognize that the whole of Scripture points to the universal *need* of salvation—even among little children. All of us are born into this world with a sin nature and are in need of redemption. All of us—*including infants who can't believe*—are lost (Luke 19:10), perishing (John 3:16), condemned (John 3:18), and under God's wrath (John 3:36).[3]

How do we know that everyone is born into this world with a sin nature? In Psalm 51:5 David said, "Surely I was sinful at birth, sinful from the time my mother conceived me." All people are "by nature objects of wrath" (Ephesians 2:3). All descendants of Adam are born in sin (1 Corinthians 15:22). "There is no one righteous, not even one" (Romans 3:10).

In view of those scriptures, we cannot say that little children are in a sinless state. We cannot say that children are in an already-redeemed state while they are yet little children. We cannot solve the issue as to whether deceased infants go to heaven by eliminating or lessening their guilt.

As theologian Robert Lightner put it so well, "Babies are beautiful and lovely, but they are also lost. They are delightful, but also depraved. They are filled with life, but they are also dead in trespasses and sins. It is not their acts of sin which place them in a state of sin. They are depraved and under divine condemnation at the moment of birth. Apart from Jesus Christ there is no salvation, neither for those who can nor for those who cannot believe."[4]

When Do Children Become "Responsible"?

Of course, there does come a time when children become morally responsible before God. Christians have often debated what age constitutes the age of accountability. Actually, it is not the same for everyone. Some children mature faster than others. Some come into an awareness of personal evil and righteousness before others do.

We read in James 4:17, "Anyone . . . who knows the good he ought to do and doesn't do it, sins." It would seem, then, that when a child truly comes into a full awareness and moral understanding of "oughts" and "shoulds," he or she at that point has reached the age of accountability.[5]

Even though the child does not become morally responsible before God until this time, he or she nevertheless has a sin nature that alienates him or her from God from the moment of birth. And whatever solution a person comes up with in regard to the issue of infant salvation must deal with this problem.

The solution, it seems to me, must be that at the moment the infant dies—*and not before*—the benefits of Jesus' atoning death on the cross are applied to him or her. And at that moment, the infant becomes saved and is immediately brought into the presence of God in heaven. This view is consistent not just with the love of God, but His holiness as well.

God's Purpose in Salvation

It is critical to realize that God's primary purpose in saving human beings is to display His wondrous grace. In Ephesians 1:7-8 we read, "In him we have redemption through his blood, the forgiveness of sins, in accordance with the riches of God's grace that he lavished on us with all wisdom and understanding."

We must ask, Would the "riches of God's grace" be displayed in "wisdom and understanding" if God sent little children to hell? I think not. It would be a cruel mockery for God to call upon infants to do—and to hold them *responsible* for doing—what they *could not* do. At a young age children simply do not have the capacity to exercise saving faith in Christ.

I believe it is the uniform testimony of Scripture that those who are not capable of making a decision to receive Jesus Christ, when they die, go to be with Christ in heaven, resting in His tender arms, enjoying the sweetness of His love. There are several factors supporting this viewpoint.

To begin, it is highly revealing that in all the descriptions of hell in the Bible, we *never* read of infants or little children there. *Not once.* Only adults capable of making decisions are seen there. Nor do we read of infants and little children standing before the Great White Throne judgment, which is the judgment of the wicked dead and the precursor to the Lake of Fire (Revelation 20:11-15).

The complete silence of Scripture regarding the presence of infants in eternal torment militates against their being there. "Not once in all the references to infants is there so much as a hint that they will ever be damned to eternal perdition after death, should they die before they have opportunity to respond to the gospel."[6]

Jesus and the Children

As we examine instances in which Christ encountered children during His earthly ministry, it seems that children have a special place in His kingdom. Consider the following moving account of Jesus' interaction with little children:

> At that time the disciples came to Jesus and asked, "Who is the greatest in the kingdom of heaven?"
>
> He called a little child and had him stand among them. And he said: "I tell you the truth, unless you change and become like little children, you will never enter the kingdom of heaven. Therefore, whoever humbles himself like this child is the greatest in the kingdom of heaven.
>
> "And whoever welcomes a little child like this in my name welcomes me. But if anyone causes one of these little ones who believe in me to sin, it would be better for him to have a large millstone hung around his neck and to be drowned in the depths of the sea. . . .
>
> "See that you do not look down on one of these little ones. For I tell you that their angels in heaven always see the face of my Father in heaven.

"What do you think? If a man owns a hundred sheep, and one of them wanders away, will he not leave the ninety-nine on the hills and go to look for the one that wandered off? And if he finds it, I tell you the truth, he is happier about that one sheep than about the ninety-nine that did not wander off. In the same way your Father in heaven is not willing that any of these little ones should be lost" (Matthew 18:1-6, 10-14).

None of the little children in Scripture opposed Jesus. *All* of them allowed Jesus to do with them as He pleased. There was no rejection on their part. And, oh, how Jesus loved them! *How very much Jesus loved the children!* I don't think there is any way someone could read this passage and conclude that it is within the realm of possibility that Jesus could condemn such little ones to hell!

The Attributes of God

God's attributes certainly relate to the issue of heaven for those who can't believe.[7] For example, God is characterized by *wisdom*. In His wisdom He chose a plan specifically designed to bring the most glory to Himself. It certainly wouldn't be glorifying to God if little infants and mentally handicapped people who died were condemned to hell because they were incapable of placing saving faith in Christ.

God is characterized by *love*. We read in 1 John 4:16, "We know and rely on the love God has for us. God is love." God not only loves, He *is* love. And it is consistent with the love of God to save those who are utterly incapable of believing in Him.*

---

*As noted earlier, God does not exercise His love at the expense of His holiness. The infant's sin problem *must* be dealt with. The solution is that at the moment the infant dies—and not before—the benefits of Jesus' atoning death on the cross are applied to him or her. And at that moment, the infant becomes saved and is immediately brought into God's presence. This view acknowledges both the love of God and His holiness.

God is characterized by *mercy* and *grace*. "Grace" refers to God's undeserved favor. "Mercy" refers to the withholding of deserved punishment. God not only shows undeserved favor to people but He also withholds deserved punishment (*see* Psalm 103:8-10). How could God be gracious and merciful if He sent those incapable of believing in Him to an eternity in hell?

God is characterized by *goodness*. Nahum 1:7 tells us that "the LORD is good." Psalm 31:19 affirms, "How great is [God's] goodness." Surely God in His goodness would not require of an infant a decision he or she could not possibly make. God in His goodness would not condemn forever someone who could not meet the requirement for salvation that He Himself set forth.

God is also characterized by *justice*. Zephaniah 3:5 says, "Morning by morning he dispenses his justice, and every new day he does not fail." Psalm 103:6 affirms, "The LORD works righteousness and justice for all the oppressed." Surely in His justice the Lord would not demand of a creature (like an infant) something that the creature was utterly incapable of (such as exercising saving faith). As Robert Lightner said, "How would God be just in refusing into His presence those who were never able to receive or reject His salvation?"[8]

It's important for us to keep in mind that, from a scriptural perspective, God's wrath comes upon people *only because they refuse God's way of escape*. Ultimately human beings choose God's wrath themselves. His wrath is poured out only on His enemies—and those who can't believe in Him are not His enemies!

J.I. Packer explains it this way: "God's wrath in the Bible is something which men *choose* for themselves. Before hell is an experience inflicted by God, it is a state for which man himself opts, by retreating from the light which God shines in his heart to lead him to Himself.'"[9] Since infants lack this ability to choose, they cannot possibly be the objects of God's wrath.

King David and His Son

King David believed that one day he would again be with his son, who had died at a very young age. In 2 Samuel 12:22-23 David said, "While the child was still alive, I fasted and wept. I thought, 'Who knows? The LORD may be gracious to me and let the child live.' But now that he is dead, why should I fast? Can I bring him back again? *I will go to him, but he will not return to me*" (emphasis added).

David displayed complete confidence that his little one was with God in heaven, and that he would one day join his son in heaven.*[10] "Life after death was a certainty for David. That he would in the future again be with his son was his firm belief. . . . David was rightly related to Jehovah, and he had no doubt that he would spend eternity with Him. Neither did he have any doubt that his infant son, taken in death before he could decide for or against his father's God, would be there also."[11]

The Basis of God's Judgment upon the Lost

Another consideration that points to the assurance of infant salvation relates to the basis of the judgment of the lost. We read this in Revelation 20:11-13:

> I saw a great white throne and him who was seated on it. Earth and sky fled from his presence, and there was no place

---

*That David was going to heaven is clear from other passages. David affirmed, "I will dwell in the house of the LORD forever" (Psalm 23:6). Just as he would dwell in the Lord's house forever, so would his young son who has died.

for them. And I saw the dead, great and small, standing before the throne, and books were opened. Another book was opened, which is the book of life. The dead were judged *according to what they had done* as recorded in the books. The sea gave up the dead that were in it, and death and Hades gave up the dead that were in them, and each person was judged *according to what he had done* (Revelation 20:11-13, emphasis added).

The basis of this judgment of the wicked is clearly deeds done while on earth. Hence, infants and mentally handicapped people cannot possibly be the objects of this judgment because they are not responsible for their deeds. Such a judgment against infants would be a travesty.

The Complete Picture

What, then, can we conclude in view of what we've just learned? I believe the scriptural position on infant salvation can be summarized in the following points:

- Every infant born into the world is born with a sin nature that causes him or her to be alienated from God.
- Every child eventually comes into moral awareness at the age of accountability.
- If a child should die before reaching the age of accountability, the benefits of Christ's death are applied to him or her *at the moment of death* (and not before), and the child is brought immediately into God's presence in heaven.
- This view is consistent with the fact that God's purpose in saving human beings is to show forth His grace and mercy.

- This view is consistent with all the attributes of God.
- This view is consistent with what Jesus said about children in the New Testament.
- This view is consistent with the fact that only adults are portrayed as being judged (and held volitionally responsible for their evil deeds) and then cast into the Lake of Fire.

We may rest with certainty, then, that children who die before coming into moral awareness—which, I firmly believe, includes *preborn* babies[12]—are resting happily and serenely in the tender arms of Jesus. They are resting securely in the sweetness of His infinite love. They are the special objects of His tender affection and care. In the words of one of the most widely sung hymns of all time:

Jesus loves the little children,
All the children of the world;
Red and yellow, black and white,
All are precious in His sight:
Jesus loves the little children of the world.

Jesus died for all the children,
All the children of the world;
Red and yellow, black and white,
All are precious in His sight:
Jesus died for all the children of the world.

> *"What do the damned endure,*
> *but despair?"*

—William Congreve (1670–1729)

7

Hell: The Infernal Destiny of the Wicked

$E_{VERYONE}$ WILL EXPERIENCE life after death. The question is not whether an individual will enter eternity, but *where he will spend it*. Those who have trusted in Christ will spend a blissful eternity with Him in heaven. Those who reject Him, however, will spend eternity apart from God in a place of great suffering. That place is hell.

In our day it has become popular to deny that there is any such place as hell. When church historian Martin Marty was preparing a lecture on this subject to be delivered at Harvard University, he couldn't find a single entry on hell when he consulted the indexes of several scholarly journals dating back over 100 years. He concluded that "hell disappeared and no one noticed."[1]

It is amazing to ponder how the word *hell* is so flippantly used in our society. People regularly use such phrases as "all hell has broken loose," "I went through hell," and "that was one hell of a game."[2] The effect of such overuse is that the word—at least for many people—no longer carries the idea of a literal place of suffering but is simply a metaphor of aggression or violence.

What Is Hell?

The Scriptures assure us that hell is a real place. But hell was not part of God's original creation, which He called "good" (Genesis 1). Hell was created later to accommodate the banishment of Satan and his fallen angels who rebelled against God (Matthew 25:41). (See my book *Angels Among Us* for a description of this sinister angelic rebellion against God prior to the creation of humankind.) People who reject Christ will join Satan and his fallen angels in this infernal place of suffering.

In the Old Testament the word "hell" translated the Hebrew word *Sheol*. *Sheol* can have different meanings in different contexts. Sometimes the word means "grave." Other times it refers to the place of departed people in contrast to the state of living people. The Old Testament portrays *Sheol* as a place of horror (Psalm 30:9) and punishment (Job 24:19).

When we get to the New Testament, we find that a number of words relate to the doctrine of hell. It seems that *Hades* is the New Testament counterpart to *Sheol* in the Old Testament. In Luke 16, the rich man, during the intermediate state, endured great suffering in Hades (verses 23-24,28).

Hades, however, is a temporary abode and will one day be cast into the Lake of Fire. In the future, the wicked evildoers in Hades will be raised from the dead and judged at the Great White Throne judgment. They will then be cast into the Lake of Fire, which will be their permanent place of suffering throughout all eternity.

Another Greek word related to the concept of hell is *Gehenna* (Matthew 10:28). This word has an interesting history. For several generations in ancient Israel, atrocities were committed in the Valley of Ben Hinnom—atrocities that included human sacrifices, even the sacrifice of children (2 Chronicles 28:3; 33:6; Jeremiah 32:35). These unfortunate victims were sacrificed to the false Moabite god Molech. Jeremiah appropriately called this valley "the Valley of Slaughter" (Jeremiah 7:32).

Eventually the valley became a public rubbish dump into which all the filth in Jerusalem was poured. Not only garbage but also the bodies of dead animals and criminals were thrown on the heap, where they—like everything else in the dump—would perpetually burn. The valley was a place where fires never stopped burning. And there was always a good meal for a hungry worm.

This place, in Hebrew, was originally called *Ge[gen]hinnom* ("the valley of the son[s] of Hinnom"). It was eventually shortened to the name Ge-Hinnom. The Greek translation of this Hebrew phrase is Gehenna.[3] It became an appropriate and graphic term for the reality of hell. Jesus Himself used the word 11 times in reference to the eternal place of suffering reserved for unredeemed humanity.

A final word related to hell is *Tartaros* (2 Peter 2:4). This word appears only one time in the Bible and refers to a place where certain fallen angels (demons) are confined. Most fallen angels are free to roam the earth, doing their destructive damage wherever they find opportunity. But these imprisoned fallen angels are not free to roam, apparently because they committed an especially heinous sin against God in the past.

Biblical Descriptions of Hell

The Scriptures use a variety of words to describe the horrors of hell—including fire, fiery furnace, unquenchable fire, the lake of burning sulfur, the Lake of Fire, everlasting contempt, perdition, the place of weeping and gnashing of teeth, eternal punishment, darkness, the wrath to come, exclusion, torments, damnation, condemnation, retribution, woe, and the second death. Though it is not a pleasant task to focus on such horror, we will examine some of these descriptions so that we can fully grasp the biblical portrait of hell.

The Lake of Burning Sulfur/The Lake of Fire

In Revelation 19:20 we read that the beast and the false prophet—two malevolent foes who come into power during the future tribulation period—will be "thrown alive into the fiery lake of burning sulfur." This will take place *before* the beginning of Christ's millennial kingdom—that 1,000-year reign of Christ following His second coming. During this reign, Christ will physically rule on earth.

What is sobering to realize is that at the end of the millennial kingdom—1,000 years *after* the beast and false prophet were thrown into the lake of burning sulfur—the devil will be "thrown into the lake of burning sulfur, where the beast and the false prophet had been thrown. *They will be tormented day and night for ever and ever*" (Revelation 20:10, emphasis added).

Notice that the beast and false prophet are not burned up or annihilated at the time the devil is thrown into the lake of burning sulfur. "They" are *still burning* after 1,000 years. These sinister beings, along with unbelievers from all the ages of mankind, will be tormented day and night forever (Revelation 20:14-15).

Eternal Fire

Jesus often referred to the final destiny of the wicked as "eternal fire." For example, Jesus warned, "If your hand or your foot causes you to sin cut it off and throw it away. It is better for you to enter life maimed or crippled than to have two hands or two feet and be thrown into eternal fire" (Matthew 18:8).

Following His second coming, when He separates the sheep (believers) from the goats (unbelievers), Jesus will say to the goats, "Depart from me, you who are cursed, into the eternal fire prepared for the devil and his angels" (Matthew 25:41).

This verse reveals an important fact: The "eternal fire" (or the Lake of Fire) was not originally created for man. Rather it was created for the devil and his host of fallen angels (demons). But fallen man will join the fallen angels in this horrendous place of suffering.

What precisely is the "fire" of hell? Some people believe it is a literal fire. And, indeed, that may very well be the case.

Other people believe "fire" is used metaphorically to express the great wrath of God. Scripture tells us, "The LORD your God is a consuming fire, a jealous God" (Deuteronomy 4:24). "God is a consuming fire" (Hebrews 12:29). "His wrath is poured out like fire" (Nahum 1:6). "Who can stand when he appears? For he will be like a refiner's fire" (Malachi 3:2). God Himself said, "My wrath will break out and burn like fire because of the evil you have done—burn with no one to quench it" (Jeremiah 4:4). How awful is the fiery wrath of God!

Fiery Furnace

Scripture also refers to the destiny of the wicked as the "fiery furnace." Jesus said that at the end of the age the holy angels will gather all evildoers and "throw them into the fiery furnace, where there will be weeping and gnashing of teeth" (Matthew 13:42).

There is a difference between fiery furnaces on earth and the fiery furnace of hell. On earth, when a person throws debris into a furnace, the debris is utterly consumed. It turns to ashes. That is not the case for people who suffer eternally in hell, for they never turn to ashes. They are not annihilated. This is a terrible truth to ponder, but the Scriptures clearly say that the wicked suffer *eternally* in hell (Mark 9:47-48).

What is meant by "weeping and gnashing of teeth"? "Weeping" carries the idea of "wailing, not merely with tears, but with every outward expression of grief."[4] This weeping will be caused by the environment, the company, the remorse and guilt, and the shame that is part and parcel of hell.

People gnash their teeth when they are angry. In his well-received book *Whatever Happened to Hell?* British evangelist John Blanchard says, "The wicked will be angry at the things which gave them pleasure on earth but now give them pain in hell; angry at the sins that wrecked their lives; angry at themselves for being who they are; angry at Satan and his helpers for producing the temptations which led them into sin; and, even while compelled to acknowledge his glory and goodness, angry at God for condemning them to this dreadful state."[5]

Destruction

Jesus warned in Matthew 7:13, "Enter through the narrow gate. For wide is the gate and broad is the road that leads to destruction, and many enter through it." The ultimate "destruction" to which Jesus refers is the destruction that is wrought in hell.

Second Thessalonians 1:8-9 tells us, "He will punish those who do not know God and do not obey the gospel of our

Lord Jesus. They will be punished *with everlasting destruction* and shut out from the presence of the Lord and from the majesty of his power" (emphasis added).

The Greek word translated "destruction" in this verse carries the meaning "sudden ruin," or "loss of all that gives worth to existence." The word refers not to annihilation but rather indicates separation from God and a loss of everything worthwhile in life. Just as "endless life" belongs to Christians, so does "endless destruction" belong to people opposed to Christ.[6]

Eternal Punishment

Jesus affirmed that the wicked "will go away to eternal punishment, but the righteous to eternal life" (Matthew 25:46). Notice that the eternality of God's punishment of the wicked *equals* the eternality of the eternal life given to the righteous. *One is just as long as the other.* This points to the "forever" nature of the punishment of the wicked. It never ceases.

The eternal nature of this punishment is emphasized all throughout Scripture. The fire of hell, for example, is called "the fire that never shall be quenched" (Mark 9:43 KJV); the worm of the wicked "does not die" (Mark 9:48); and the "smoke of their [the sinners'] torment rises for ever and ever" (Revelation 14:11).

Of particular significance is the reference to the devil, the beast, and the false prophet being tormented in the Lake of Fire "for ever and ever" (Revelation 20:10). This is significant because the Greek word translated "for ever and ever" is used elsewhere in Revelation to talk about the endless worship of God (Revelation 1:6; 4:9; 5:13). The word is also used to speak of the endless life of God (4:10; 10:6). Further, the word is used in reference to Christ's endless kingdom (11:15).[7] The suffering of evildoers, then, is endless . . . endless . . . endless.

Exclusion from God's Presence

Unquestionably the greatest pain suffered by people in hell is that they are forever excluded from the presence of God. If ecstatic joy is found in the presence of God (Psalm 16:11), then utter dismay is found in His absence.

At the future judgment some people will claim that they were Christians and say that they served Christ during their years on earth. But Christ will say to them, "I don't know you or where you come from. *Away from me*, all you evildoers!" (Luke 13:27, emphasis added). Such individuals will find themselves forever excluded from God's presence. They will be "shut out from the presence of the Lord and from the majesty of his power" (2 Thessalonians 1:9).

At the judgment of the sheep (believers) and goats (unbelievers), Christ will command the goats, "*Depart from me*, you who are cursed, into the eternal fire prepared for the devil and his angels" (Matthew 25:31-46, emphasis added). What utterly horrific words to hear from the lips of the King of kings and Lord of lords: "Depart from me . . ."

Degrees of Punishment in Hell

Though this may come as a surprise to some people, the Scriptures clearly indicate that there are degrees of punishment in hell. Certainly an Adolf Hitler will suffer eternally much more than a Christ-rejecting moralist. The degree of punishment will be commensurate with a person's sin against the light which that person has received.

The following passages affirm that there will be degrees of punishment in hell:

- *Matthew 10:15*—"I tell you the truth, it will be *more bearable* for Sodom and Gomorrah on the day of judgment than for that town."
- *Matthew 16:27*—"The Son of Man is going to come in his Father's glory with his angels, and then he will *reward each person according to what he has done.*"
- *Luke 12:47-48*—"That servant who knows his master's will and does not get ready or does not do what his master wants will be *beaten with many blows.* But the one who does not know and does things deserving punishment will be *beaten with few blows.* From everyone who has been given much, much will be demanded; and from the one who has been entrusted with much, much more will be asked."
- *Revelation 20:12-13*—"Another book was opened, which is the book of life. The dead were judged *according to what they had done* as recorded in the books. The sea gave up the dead that were in it, and death and Hades gave up the dead that were in them, and each person was judged *according to what he had done.*"
- *Revelation 22:12*—"Behold, I am coming soon! My reward is with me, and *I will give to everyone according to what he has done.*"

Clearly, then, the wicked will be judged according to what they did while on earth. Some people will be punished more severely than others because of the more heinous wrongdoings they committed. The biblical God is a God of justice.

Whether a person is "beaten with few blows" or "beaten with many blows" in hell, it's important to recognize that ultimately, *all* the occupants of hell end up there according to their own will. The redeemed are the people who say to God, "Your will be done." However, as C.S. Lewis pointed out in his book *The Great Divorce*, the condemned who populate hell are the people to whom God finally says, "*Your* will be done."

Indeed, these individuals reject the only thing that would keep them out of hell: believing in Jesus Christ as Lord and Savior. Any human soul that freely refuses the one Source of all life and joy *must* find death and misery in hell as its inevitable punishment.

False Views of Hell

Because hell is so horrible and frightening, many people have sought to explain it away or soften what they consider to be severe views of hell. False views of hell include annihilationism, universalism, the doctrine of purgatory, and reincarnation. Let's briefly test these views against the Scriptures.

Annihilationism

The doctrine of annihilationism teaches that man was created immortal. But people who continue in sin and reject Christ are, by a positive act of God, deprived of the gift of immortality and are ultimately destroyed.

Another view, called "conditional immortality," argues that immortality is not a natural endowment of man, but is rather a gift of God in Christ only to people who believe. The person who does not accept Christ is ultimately annihilated and loses all consciousness. Some of the advocates of these doctrines teach a limited duration of conscious suffering for the wicked after death, after which time they are annihilated.

There are many Bible passages that refute annihilationism. For illustration purposes, we will select only one primary passage—Matthew 25:46: "They will go away to eternal punishment, but the righteous to eternal life."

By no stretch of the imagination can the punishment spoken of in Matthew 25:46 be defined as a nonsuffering extinction of consciousness. Indeed, if actual suffering is lacking, then so is punishment. Let us be clear on this: *punishment entails suffering.* And suffering necessarily entails consciousness.[8]

Bible scholar John Gerstner tells us that "one can exist and not be punished; but no one can be punished and not exist. Annihilation means the obliteration of existence and anything that pertains to existence, such as punishment. Annihilation avoids punishment, rather than encountering it."[9]

How do we know that the punishment mentioned in Matthew 25:46 does not include an extinction of consciousness and annihilation? There are many evidences. For example, consider the fact that there are no *degrees* of annihilation. A person is either annihilated or not. The Scriptures, by contrast, teach that there will be degrees of punishment on the day of judgment (Matthew 10:15; 11:21-24; 16:27; Luke 12:47-48; John 15:22; Hebrews 10:29; Revelation 20:11-15; 22:12).[10]

The very fact that people will suffer varying degrees of punishment in hell shows that annihilation or the extinction of consciousness is not taught in Matthew 25:46 or anywhere else in Scripture. These are incompatible concepts.

Moreover, we cannot deny that for a person who is suffering excruciating pain, the extinction of his or her consciousness would actually be a *blessing*—not a punishment (cf. Luke 23:30-31; Revelation 9:6). Any honest seeker after truth must admit that a person cannot define "eternal punishment" as an extinction of consciousness.

By definition, torment cannot be anything *but* conscious torment. We cannot torment a tree, a rock, or a house. By its very nature, being tormented requires consciousness. Bible scholar Alan Gomes correctly points out that "a punishment [such as torment] that is not felt is not a punishment. It is an odd use of language to speak of an insensate (i.e., unfeeling), inanimate object receiving punishment. To say, 'I punished my car for not starting by slowly plucking out its sparkplug wires, one by one,' would evoke laughter, not serious consideration."[11] Punishment, then, entails consciousness.

A critical point to make about the punishment described in Matthew 25:46 is that it is said to be *eternal*. There is no way that annihilationism or an extinction of consciousness can be forced into that passage. Indeed, the Greek adjective *aionion* in that verse literally means "everlasting, without end." As noted earlier, this same adjective is predicated of God (the "eternal" God) in 1 Timothy 1:17, Romans 16:26, Hebrews 9:14, 13:8, and Revelation 4:9. *The punishment of the wicked is just as eternal as our eternal God.*

Universalism

Universalism states that sooner or later all people will be saved. This position believes that the concepts of hell and punishment are inconsistent with a loving God.

The older form of universalism, originating in the second century, taught that salvation would come after a temporary period of punishment. The newer form of universalism declares that all men *are now* saved, though all do not realize it. Therefore the job of the preacher and the missionary is to tell people they are already saved. Certain Bible passages—John 12:32, Philippians 2:10-11, and 1 Timothy 2:4—are typically twisted out of context in support of universalism.

Such passages, interpreted properly, *do not* support universalism:

- John 12:32 says that Christ's work on the cross *makes possible* the salvation of both Jews and Gentiles. Notice, however, that the Lord—in the *same passage*—warned of judgment to those who reject Christ (verse 48).
- Philippians 2:10-11 assures us that someday all people will acknowledge that Jesus is Lord, but they won't necessarily confess that he is Savior. (Even those in hell will have to acknowledge Christ's lordship.)
- First Timothy 2:4 expresses God's *desire* that all people be saved, but does not *promise* that will happen. This divine desire is realized only in people who exercise faith in Christ.

The Scriptures consistently categorize people into one of two classes (*saved/unsaved*, also called *believers/unbelievers*), and portray the final destiny of every person as being one of two realities (*heaven* or *hell*).

- In Matthew 13:30 Jesus, in a parable, said, "Let both [tares and wheat] grow together until the harvest. At that time I will tell the harvesters: First collect the weeds and tie them in bundles to be burned; then gather the wheat and bring it into my barn." Here unbelievers and believers are spoken of as *tares* and *wheat*—two classes of people.

- In Matthew 13:49 Jesus said, "This is how it will be at the end of the age. The angels will come and separate the wicked from the righteous." Again, two classes are mentioned—unbelievers and believers, who are spoken of as the *wicked* and the *righteous.*
- In Matthew 25:32 Jesus said that following His second coming, "All the nations will be gathered before him, and he will separate the people one from another as a shepherd separates the sheep from the goats." Here, believers and unbelievers are differentiated by the terms "sheep" and "goats." The sheep will enter into God's kingdom (verse 34) and inherit eternal life (verse 46). The goats will go into eternal punishment (verse 46).
- In Luke 16:26 we find Abraham, in the afterlife, telling the unsaved rich man, "Between us and you a great chasm has been fixed, so that those who want to go from here to you cannot, nor can anyone cross over from there to us." According to this account, Hades apparently had two compartments: "paradise" for the saved, and "torments" for the unsaved—and these compartments were separated by a great chasm or gulf.

Clearly, then, the Scriptures speak of two classes of people (the saved and the unsaved) and two possible destinies (heaven for the saved; hell for the unsaved). And every person will end up in one of those places based upon whether or not he or she placed saving faith in Christ during his or her time on earth (John 3:18; *see also* Mark 16:16).

Purgatory

The Roman Catholic Church teaches that people who are perfect at death are admitted to heaven. Those who are not perfectly cleansed and are still tainted with the guilt of venial sins, however, do not go to heaven. Rather, they go to purgatory, where they allegedly go through a process of cleansing (or "purging"). These souls are oppressed with a sense of deprivation and suffer certain pain. How long they stay in purgatory—and how much suffering they undergo while there—depends upon their particular state of sin.

Roman Catholics also teach that a person's time in purgatory may be shortened, and his pains alleviated, by the faithful prayers and good works of people who are still alive. The sacrifice of the Mass is viewed as especially important in this regard. Catholics find support for this doctrine in the apocryphal book 2 Maccabees 12:42-45.

That purgatory is a false doctrine is easy to prove from the Scriptures. When Jesus died on the cross, He said "It is finished" (John 19:30). Jesus completed the work of redemption at the cross. In His high priestly prayer to the Father, He said, "I have brought you glory on earth by *completing the work* you gave me to do" (John 17:4, emphasis added). Hebrews 10:14 emphatically declares, "By one sacrifice he has made perfect forever those who are being made holy." Hence, people who believe in Christ are "made perfect" forever; no further "purging" is necessary. First John 1:7 says, "The blood of Jesus, his Son, purifies us from *all* sin." Romans 8:1 says, "There is *now* no condemnation for those who are in Christ Jesus."

Jesus took care of "purging" our sins by His work of salvation at the cross. Hebrews 1:3 affirms, "After he had provided purification for sins, he sat down at the right hand of the Majesty in heaven." Jesus provided *full* purification for our sins.

Reincarnation

Today approximately 30 million Americans (one in four) believe in reincarnation. The word *reincarnation* literally means to "come again in the flesh." The process of reincarnation—continual rebirths in human bodies*—allegedly continues until the soul has reached a state of perfection and merges back with its source (God, or the "Universal Soul").

A person's lot in life, according to those who believe in reincarnation, is based on the law of karma. This law says that if bad things happen in your life, this is an outworking of bad karma. If good things happen in your life, this is an outworking of good karma.

"Karma" refers to the "debt" a soul accumulates because of good or bad actions committed during a person's life (or past lives). If a person accumulates good karma by performing good actions, he or she will be reincarnated in a desirable state. If a person accumulates bad karma, he or she will be reincarnated in a less desirable state. In Shirley MacLaine's book *Out on a Limb* we are told, "Reincarnation is like show business. You just keep doing it until you get it right."[12]

Some people twist the Scriptures and say that Jesus Himself taught reincarnation or "cyclical rebirth." In Matthew 11:14, for example, Jesus said, "If you are willing to accept it, [John the Baptist] is the Elijah who was to come." Likewise, in John 3:3 Jesus said, "I tell you the truth, no one can see the kingdom of God unless he is born again."

But these passages, rightly interpreted, do not support reincarnation. Matthew 11:14 does not teach that John the Baptist was a reincarnation of Elijah. Luke 1:17, an important cross-reference, tells us that the ministry of John the Baptist

---

*Note that some reincarnationists believe a person can be reborn as an animal.

was carried out "in the *spirit and power* of Elijah" (emphasis added). Moreover, reincarnationists conveniently forget that John the Baptist, when asked if he was Elijah, flatly answered, "No"! (John 1:21).

As for Jesus' words about being "born again" in John 3:3, the context clearly shows that Jesus was referring to a *spiritual* rebirth or regeneration. In fact, the phrase "born again" carries the idea of "born from above" and can even be translated that way. Jesus clarified what he meant by affirming that "flesh gives birth to flesh, but the Spirit gives birth to spirit" (verse 6).

There are other Scriptures that clearly debunk the notion of reincarnation. Hebrews 9:27 tells us that "man is destined to die once, and after that to face judgment." Each human being lives once as a mortal on earth, dies once, and then faces judgment. He does not have a second chance by reincarnating into another body. Second Corinthians 5:8 indicates that at death the Christian immediately goes into the presence of the Lord, not into another body. Luke 16:19-31 tells us that at death, unbelievers go to a place of suffering, not into another body.

We must also remember that Jesus taught that people decide their eternal destiny in a single lifetime (Matthew 25:46). This is precisely why the apostle Paul emphasized that "*now* is the day of salvation" (2 Corinthians 6:2).

Furthermore, Jesus taught the concept of resurrection, not reincarnation. In fact, He predicted His own resurrection early in His public ministry (John 2:19). And after Jesus rose from the dead, He appeared to some disciples and said, "Look at my hands and my feet. It is I myself! Touch me and see; a ghost does not have flesh and bones, as you see I have" (Luke 24:39). Jesus resurrected *in the same body that went into the tomb*. His body even retained the scars and wounds that His hands, feet, and side received during the crucifixion (John 20:27).

In addition to biblically refuting reincarnation, we must also point to some of the practical problems involved in the theory of reincarnation. For example, we must ask, Why does a person get punished (via "bad karma") for something he or she cannot remember having done in a previous life? Moreover, if the purpose of karma is to rid humanity of its selfish desires (as reincarnationists say), then why has there not been a noticeable improvement in human nature after all the millennia of reincarnations on earth?

Finally, if reincarnation and the law of karma are so beneficial on a practical level, as reincarnationists claim, then how do they explain the immense and ever-worsening social and economic problems—including widespread poverty, starvation, disease, and horrible suffering—in India, where reincarnation has been systematically taught throughout its history?

Can We Be Happy in Heaven Knowing There Is a Hell?

This is a difficult question to answer. In fact, on this side of eternity, we do not have all the wisdom and insight we need to fully answer it. But there are some scriptural considerations that can help us to have a right perspective.

First, God Himself has promised that He will take away all pain and remove all our tears (Revelation 21:4). All matters are in His hands. We can rest assured that He has the power and ability to do as He has promised. It is a fact that we will be happy in heaven. God has promised it. Charles Spurgeon once said, with good reason, that the resurrection body will not have tear glands because they will not be necessary.

Second, we will be aware of the full justice of God's decisions. We will clearly see that those who are in hell are there precisely because they rejected God's only provision for escaping hell. They are those to whom God ultimately says, "*Thy* will be done."

Third, we learned in this chapter that there are degrees of punishment in hell, just as there are degrees of reward in heaven. This gives us an assurance that the Hitlers of human history will be in a much greater state of suffering than, for example, a non-Christian moralist.

God is perfectly wise and just. He knows what He is doing! You and I can rest with quiet assurance in His wisdom and justice.

> *"In the choir of life, it's easy to fake the words. But someday each of us will have to sing solo before God."*

—Anonymous

8

The Judgment of Humankind

John Wesley, in one of his famous sermons, commented, "Every man shall give an account of his own works, a full and true account of all that he ever did while alive, whether it was good or evil."[1]

Such words are needed in times like these. It seems that few people today govern their actions with a view to being held accountable for them at a future judgment. Though many people prefer to ignore any mention of the subject, the fact remains that *every* human being—both Christian and non-Christian—will face judgment.

As we will see in a moment, however, the purpose of the believer's judgment is altogether different from that of the unbeliever's judgment. The believer is judged not in connection with his or her salvation (which is absolutely secure), but in regard to receiving or losing rewards from God. The unbeliever, in contrast, is judged as a precursor to his being cast into the Lake of Fire. We will examine both of these judgments in this chapter.

First, however, we must firmly establish in our minds that God is, in fact, a God of judgment. In recent years this idea has fallen out of favor. Most people prefer to focus almost exclusively on the love of God. Certainly it is true that God *is* a God of love. But He is also a holy and righteous Judge. This has always been true of Him.

In his modern classic *Knowing God,* popular writer J.I. Packer said this:

> The reality of divine judgment, as a fact, is set forth on page after page of Bible history. God judged Adam and Eve, expelling them from the Garden and pronouncing curses on their future earthly life (Genesis 3). God judged the corrupt world of Noah's day, sending a flood to destroy mankind (Genesis 6–8). God judged Sodom and Gomorrah, engulfing them in a volcanic catastrophe (Genesis 18–19). God judged Israel's Egyptian taskmasters, just as He foretold He would (*see* Genesis 15:14), unleashing against them the terrors of the ten plagues (Exodus 7–12). God judged those who worshipped the golden calf, using the Levites as His executioners (Exodus 32:26-35). God judged Nadab and Abihu for offering Him strange fire (Leviticus 10:1ff.), as later He judged Korah, Dathan, and Abiram, who were swallowed up in an earth tremor. God judged Achan for sacrilegious thieving; he and his family were wiped out (Joshua 7). God judged Israel for unfaithfulness to Him after their entry into Canaan, causing them to fall under the dominion of other nations (Judges 2:11ff., 3:5ff., 4:1ff.).[2]

In the New Testament we find that judgment fell on the Jewish people who rejected Jesus Christ (Matthew 21:43), on Ananias and Sapphira for lying to God (Acts 5), on Herod for his self-exalting pride (Acts 12:21-23), and on Christians in Corinth who showed irreverence toward the Lord's Supper (1 Corinthians 11:29-32).

God truly is a God of judgment. If we forget or ignore this fact, we do so at our own peril. God will hold all of us accountable for the things done in this life.

Judgment Is According to the Light Given

As a foundational principle, it is important to understand that God's judgment of each person will be based upon that particular person's response to the revealed will of God. And, certainly, God will take into account that people have different degrees of knowledge about God's will (which means they will vary in their ability to fulfill that will).

Jesus spoke of this when He said, "The one who does not know and does things deserving punishment will be beaten with few blows. From everyone who has been given much, much will be demanded; and from the one who has been entrusted with much, much more will be asked" (Luke 12:48). Each person's knowledge of God's will, then, is taken into consideration at judgment. (You might want to read through Matthew 11:21-24 for a graphic illustration of this principle.)

We can rest assured that God's judgment is utterly fair. In the face of the many injustices that characterize life in the present age, we can rest in the certainty that God knows all, that He is not mocked, and that He has appointed a day in which He will judge the world in righteousness (Acts 17:31).

What About People Who Have Never Heard?

Perhaps one of the most oft-asked questions about judgment has to do with the destiny of people who have never heard the gospel of Christ. This may initially seem to pose an insurmountable problem in regard to the "fairness" of Christianity. But it does not, for, as we just noted, God always judges people according to the light given. And one truth we learn in Scripture is that God has given a certain amount of "light" to every single person in the world.

Everyone has some sense of God's law in his or her heart. As John Blanchard put it so well, everyone "has some conception of the difference between right and wrong; he approves of honesty; he responds to love and kindness; he resents it if someone steals his goods or tries to injure him. In other words, he has a conscience which passes judgment on his behavior and the behavior of others, something the Bible calls a law written on his heart."[3] Paul speaks of this law written on human hearts in Romans 2:15.

God has also given witness of Himself in the universe around us. In beholding the world and the universe, it is evident that there is someone who made them. Since the creation of the world, God's invisible qualities—His eternal power and divine nature—have been clearly seen and understood from that which He created (Romans 1:20).

We know from other Scripture verses that God is an invisible spirit (John 4:24). The physical eye cannot see Him. But His existence is clearly reflected in what He has made— the creation. The *creation,* which is visible, reveals the existence of the *Creator,* who is invisible.

Because all human beings can see the revelation of God in creation, all people—regardless of whether they've heard about Christ or read the Bible—are held accountable before God. *All are without excuse* (Romans 1:20). Their rightful condemnation, as objects of God's wrath, is justified because their choice to ignore the revelation of God in creation is indefensible (*see* Psalm 19:1-6).

At the same time, the Scriptures clearly indicate that people who respond to the limited light around them (such as God's witness of Himself in the universe) will receive further, more specific "light." This is illustrated in the life of Cornelius.

Cornelius, a Gentile, was obedient to the limited amount of "light" he had received—that is, he had been obedient to

Old Testament revelation (Acts 10:2). But he didn't have enough "light" to believe in Jesus Christ as the Savior. So God sent Peter to Cornelius's house to explain the gospel, after which time Cornelius believed in Jesus and became saved (Acts 10:44-48).

In view of these principles about God's revelation, we must not allow God's name to be impugned by people who imply that He is unfair if He judges individuals who have never heard the gospel. As we have seen, God has given a witness of Himself to *all* humanity. Moreover, God desires all people to be saved (1 Timothy 2:4) and doesn't want anyone to perish (2 Peter 3:9). He certainly takes no pleasure in the death of the unsaved (Ezekiel 18:23).

Let us remember that God is a fair Judge. "It is unthinkable that God would do wrong, that the Almighty would pervert justice" (Job 34:12). "Will not the Judge of all the earth do right?" (Genesis 18:25).

The Judgment of Believers

All believers will one day stand before the judgment seat of Christ (Romans 14:8-10). At that time, God will examine the deeds each believer did while in the body. Personal motives and intents of the heart will also be weighed.

The idea of a "judgment seat" relates to the athletic games of Paul's day. "After the races and games concluded, a dignitary or even the emperor himself took his seat on an elevated throne in the arena. One by one the winning athletes came up to the throne to receive a reward—usually a wreath of leaves, a victor's crown."[4] Similarly, there is coming a day when we who are Christians will stand before Christ the Judge and receive (or lose) rewards.

Christ will not judge all believers together in a corporate setting—like a big class being praised or scolded by a teacher. Rather, our judgment will be individual and personal. "We will *all* stand before God's judgment seat" (Romans 14:10, emphasis added). Each of us will be judged on an individual basis.

This judgment has nothing to do with whether or not the Christian will remain saved. Those who have placed faith in Christ *are* saved, and nothing threatens that. Believers are eternally secure in their salvation. The judgment of believers deals strictly with the reception or loss of rewards.

Scripture indicates that this judgment will take place immediately after the church is "raptured"* and Christ takes the saints back to heaven. No Bible verse explicitly states this, but a number of factors lead us to this conclusion.

First, many Bible scholars believe that the 24 elders in heaven (Revelation 4:1,10) represent believers—and they are portrayed as already having their crowns in heaven at the very start of the tribulation period. Moreover, when the bride of Christ (the corporate body of Christians) returns to earth with Christ at the second coming, the bride is "clothed with righteous deeds"—implying that she has already passed through judgment (Revelation 19:8).

Now, it seems to be the testimony of Scripture that some believers, at the judgment, may have a sense of deprivation and suffer some degree of forfeiture and shame. Indeed, certain rewards may be forfeited that otherwise might have been received, and this will involve a sense of loss. The fact is, Christians differ radically in holiness of conduct and faithfulness in service. God, in His justice and holiness, takes all

---

*The "rapture" is that future event—just prior to the beginning of the tribulation period—in which Christ will remove all the Christians from the world and take them to heaven. At the rapture, believers will receive their glorified resurrection bodies.

this into account. Some believers will be without shame and others *with* shame at the judgment seat of Christ.

Second John 8 warns us, "Watch out that you do not lose what you have worked for, but that you may be rewarded fully." In 1 John 2:28 we are encouraged to live such that "we may be confident and unashamed before him at his coming."

We must keep all this in perspective, however. Christ's coming for us at the rapture and the prospect of living eternally with Him should give each of us joy. And our joy will last for all eternity. How can we reconcile this forever joy with the possible loss of reward and perhaps even some level of shame at the judgment seat of Christ?

I think Herman Hoyt's explanation is the best I've found:

> The judgment seat of Christ might be compared to a commencement ceremony. At graduation there is some measure of disappointment and remorse that one did not do better and work harder. However, at such an event the overwhelming emotion is joy, not remorse. The graduates do not leave the auditorium weeping because they did not earn better grades. Rather, they are thankful that they have been graduated, and they are grateful for what they did achieve. To overdo the sorrow aspect of the judgment seat of Christ is to make heaven hell. To underdo the sorrow aspect is to make faithfulness inconsequential.[5]

At the judgment seat of Christ, all earthly inequities will be righted *once for all*—including inequities committed among Christians. Can you think of a time when you saw a believer suffer wrongfully at the hands of a fellow believer? Can you think of a time when a humble Christian suffered cruelty at the hands of a proud and carnal believer? Such injustices as these will be vindicated on that day of judgment. The Lord "will bring to light what is hidden in darkness and will expose the motives of men's hearts" (1 Corinthians 4:5).

Tried by Fire

In 1 Corinthians 3:11-15 we read,

> No one can lay any foundation other than the one already laid, which is Jesus Christ. If any man builds on this foundation using gold, silver, costly stones, wood, hay or straw, his work will be shown for what it is, because the Day will bring it to light. It will be revealed with fire, and the fire will test the quality of each man's work. If what he has built survives, he will receive his reward. If it is burned up, he will suffer loss; he himself will be saved, but only as one escaping through the flames.

Notice that the materials Paul mentions in this passage are combustible in increasing degrees. Obviously the hay and straw are the most combustible. Then comes wood. And finally, precious metals and stones cannot burn.

It also seems clear that some of these materials are useful for building while others are not. If you construct a house made of hay or straw, it surely will not stand long. (And it can burn to the ground very easily.) But a house constructed with solid materials such as stones and metals will stand and last a long time.

What do these building materials represent? Pastor Douglas Connelly insightfully suggests that "gold, silver, and costly stones refer to the fruit of the Spirit in our lives; they refer to Christ-honoring motives and godly obedience and transparent integrity. Wood, hay, and straw are perishable things—carnal attitudes, sinful motives, pride-filled actions, selfish ambition."[6]

In Scripture, fire often symbolizes the holiness of God (Dueteronomy 4:24; Hebrews 12:29). Fire also portrays God's judgment upon that which His holiness has condemned (Genesis 19:24; Mark 9:43-48). God, then, will examine our works, and they will be tested against the fire of His holiness. If our works are built with good materials—like precious metals and stones—they will stand. But if our works are built with less valuable materials—wood, hay, or straw—they will burn up.

Perhaps the illustration is intended to communicate that those works performed with a view to glorifying God are the works that will stand. Those works done with the desire to glorify self, done in the flesh, are those that will be burned up.

Apparently some believers will suffer such loss at the judgment seat of Christ that practically all—*if not all*—of their works will go up in flames. Paul describes this person as being saved, "but only as one escaping through the flames" (1 Corinthians 3:15). Theologian Merrill F. Unger explains it this way:

> Imagine yourself waking out of sleep to find your house ablaze. You have no time to save a thing. You flee with only the night clothes on your back. Even these are singed away by the flames that engulf you. You escape with literally nothing but your life. . . . In this fashion believers who have lived carnally and carelessly or who have worked for self and self-interest instead of for the Lord will find that all their works have been burned up. They shall have no reward. No trophies to lay at Jesus' feet! No crowns to rejoice in that day of judgment![7]

Running the Race

In 1 Corinthians 9:24-27 we read,

> Do you not know that in a race all the runners run, but only one gets the prize? Run in such a way as to get the prize. Everyone who competes in the games goes into strict training.

They do it to get a crown that will not last; but we do it to get a crown that will last forever. Therefore I do not run like a man running aimlessly; I do not fight like a man beating the air. No, I beat my body and make it my slave so that after I have preached to others, I myself will not be disqualified for the prize.

Paul's concern here was that he not be disapproved of at the judgment seat of Christ. He didn't want to do anything that would render him unworthy to receive rewards from his beloved Lord.

Understanding the athletic events of Paul's day helps us to better grasp Paul's point. Among the Greeks, one of the most thrilling sport events was the Isthmian games, which were celebrated every two years in the city of Corinth. Two of the games at this event were footracing and boxing.

In footracing, a person must engage in a sustained effort to win the prize. Applying this principle to spiritual truth, Paul said that "in a race all the runners run," but only one person wins the award. Therefore, Paul says, "run in such a way as to get the prize." *That is a call to live a sustained life of faithfulness.*

In boxing, a person must be self-controlled and well trained if he wants to render well-landed blows to the opponent. Applying that to spiritual truth, Paul said he directed well-aimed blows at his own body to keep it under subjection. *That is a call to guard against carnal desires.*

Those who won the Greek games received a mere "crown that will not last"—a wreath made of wild olive leaves and parsley, which fade over time. This contrasts with the imperishable awards that will be handed out to faithful Christians at Christ's judgment seat.

The Judgment of Our Actions

The Christian's judgment will focus on his personal steward-ship of the gifts, talents, opportunities, and responsibilities given to him in this life. The very character of each Christian's life and service will be laid bare under the unerr-ing and omniscient vision of Christ, whose "eyes [are] like blazing fire" (Revelation 1:14).

Many Scripture verses reveal that each of our actions will be judged before the Lord. The psalmist said to the Lord, "Surely you will reward each person according to what he has done" (Psalm 62:12; cf. Matthew 16:27). In Ephesians 6:8 we read that the Lord "will reward everyone for whatever good he does, whether he is slave or free."

Christ's judgment of our actions will be infallible. There will be no confusion on His part. His understanding of the circumstances under which we committed our actions on earth will be complete. As John Wesley once said, "God will . . . bring to light every circumstance that accompanied each word and action. He will judge whether they lessened or increased the goodness or badness of them."[8]

The Judgment of Our Thoughts

At the judgment seat of Christ, it won't just be our *actions* that will come under scrutiny. The Lord will also judge our *thoughts*. In Jeremiah 17:10 God said, "I the LORD search the heart and examine the mind, to reward a man according to his conduct, according to what his deeds deserve." The Lord "will bring to light what is hidden in darkness and will ex-pose the motives of men's hearts" (1 Corinthians 4:5). The Lord is the One "who searches hearts and minds" (Revelation 2:23).

It is with verses like these in mind that John Wesley wrote, "In that day, every inward working of the human soul will be discovered—every appetite, passion, inclination, and affection, with all the various combinations of them, and every temper and disposition that constitutes the whole complex character of each individual. Who was righteous, who was unrighteous, and in what degree every action, or person, or character was either good or evil will be seen clearly and infallibly."[9]

The Judgment of Our Words

Finally, the believer's judgment will include all the words he has spoken. Christ once said that "men will have to give account on the day of judgment for every careless word they have spoken" (Matthew 12:36). This is an important aspect of judgment, for tremendous damage can be done through the human tongue *(see* James 3:1-12).

John Blanchard reminds us that "if even our careless words are carefully recorded, how can we bear the thought that our calculated boastful claims, the cutting criticisms, the off-color jokes, and the unkind comments—will also be taken into account. Even our whispered asides and words spoken in confidence or when we thought we were 'safe' will be heard again."[10]

Rewards and Crowns

What kinds of rewards will believers receive at the judgment seat of Christ? Scripture often speaks of them in terms of crowns that we wear. In fact, there are a number of different crowns that symbolize the various spheres of achievement and award in the Christian life.

The *crown of life* is given to those who persevere under trial, and especially to those who suffer to the point of death (James 1:12; Revelation 2:10). The *crown of glory* is given to those who faithfully and sacrificially minister God's Word to the flock (1 Peter 5:4). The *crown incorruptible* is given to those who win the race of temperance and self-control (1 Corinthians 9:25 KJV). The *crown of righteousness* is given to those who long for the second coming of Christ (2 Timothy 4:8).

It is intriguing that in Revelation 4:10 we find believers casting their crowns before the throne of God in an act of worship and adoration. This teaches us something very important. Clearly the crowns (as rewards) are bestowed on us not for our own glory but ultimately for the glory of God. We are told elsewhere in Scripture that believers are redeemed to bring glory to God (1 Corinthians 6:20). It seems that the act of placing our crowns before the throne of God would be one way of bringing glory to Him.

Here's something else to think about: The greater reward or crown a believer has received, the greater capacity he or she has to bring glory to the Creator. The lesser reward or crown a person has received, the lesser is his or her capacity to bring glory to the Creator. Because of the different rewards handed out at the judgment seat of Christ, believers will have differing capacities to bring glory to God.

Still, we shouldn't take this to mean that certain believers will have a sense of lack throughout eternity. After all, each believer will be glorifying God *to the fullness of his capacity* in the next life. Each one of us, then, will be able to "declare the praises of him who called [us] out of darkness into his wonderful light" (1 Peter 2:9).[11]

The Judgment of Unbelievers

Unlike believers, whose judgment deals only with rewards and loss of rewards, unbelievers face a horrific judgment that leads to their being cast into the Lake of Fire. This latter judgment is called the Great White Throne judgment (Revelation 20:11-15). Christ is the divine Judge, and those who are judged are the unsaved dead of all time. The judgment will take place at the end of the millennial kingdom, Christ's 1000-year reign on planet earth.

The people who face Christ at this time will be judged on the basis of their works (Revelation 20:12-13). It is critical to understand that these people face this judgment because they are *already unsaved*. This judgment will not separate believers from unbelievers, for all the people who are present before the Great White Throne will have already made the choice *during their lifetimes* to reject God. Once they are before the divine Judge, they are judged according to their works not only to justify their condemnation but also to determine the degree to which they should be punished throughout eternity.

When Christ opens the Book of Life, He will not see the names of people who will be at the Great White Throne judgment. Their names do not appear in the *Book* of Life because they have rejected the *source* of life—Jesus Christ. Because they rejected the source of life, they are cast into the Lake of Fire—which constitutes the "second death" and involves eternal separation from God.

Resurrected Unto Judgment

The people who participate in the Great White Throne judgment are resurrected unto judgment. Jesus Himself affirmed that "a time is coming when all who are in their graves will hear his voice and come out—those who have done good will rise to live, and those who have done evil will rise to be condemned" (John 5:28-29).

Realize, however, that Jesus is not teaching that there is just one general resurrection that will take place at the end of time. Contrary to this idea, the Scriptures indicate that there are two resurrections—the first resurrection and the second resurrection (Revelation 20:5-6,11-15). The first resurrection is the resurrection of Christians, while the second resurrection is the resurrection of the wicked.

Now, the term "first resurrection" refers to *all* the resurrections of the righteous, even though they are widely separated in time. There is one resurrection of the righteous at the rapture (before the tribulation period); another at the end of the tribulation period; and still another at the end of the 1000-year millennial kingdom (1 Thessalonians 4:16; Revelation 20:4). They all are "first" in the sense of being before the second (final) resurrection of the wicked. Accordingly, the term "first resurrection" applies to all the resurrections of the saints regardless of when they occur, including the resurrection of Christ Himself.

The second resurrection is an awful spectacle. All the unsaved people of all time will be resurrected at the end of Christ's millennial kingdom, judged at the Great White Throne, and then cast alive into the Lake of Fire (Revelation 20:11-15). "Men will be given bodies that will last forever, but bodies that are sinful and subject to pain and suffering. Like the Devil and his angels, they will exist forever in the lake of fire."[12]

Degrees of Punishment

The Scriptures indicate that *all* the people who appear at the Great White Throne judgment have a horrible destiny ahead.

Indeed, their future generally will involve weeping and gnashing of teeth (Matthew 13:41-42), condemnation (Matthew 12:36-37), destruction (Philippians 1:28), eternal punishment (Matthew 25:46), separation from God's presence (2 Thessalonians 1:8-9), and trouble and distress (Romans 2:9). And, as noted in the previous chapter, these people will suffer varying degrees of punishment. The severity of punishment will be determined at the Great White Throne judgment when Christ examines each person with His penetrating eyes.

Common observation shows that unsaved people vary as much in their quality of life as saved people do. Some saved people are spiritual and charitable, and other saved people are carnal and unloving. Some unbelievers are terribly evil (like Hitler), while others—such as unbelieving moralists—are much less evil.

Just as believers differ in how they respond to God's law and hence in the reward they will receive in heaven, so also do unbelievers differ in their response to God's law and hence the degree of their punishment in hell. Just as there are degrees of reward in heaven, so also are there degrees of punishment in hell.

Why Judgment Matters

The fact that all of us will one day be judged should have a profound effect on the way we live. There is little else that could so motivate us to do good and deter us from evil than a strong conviction that the divine Judge is standing at the door and we are shortly to stand before Him. Indeed, as a great eighteenth-century saint said, "No better motive can be found to guarantee a steady pursuit of solid virtue and a uniform walk in justice, mercy, and truth."[13] Selah!

> *"We now have sufficient scientific grounds for asserting that there is a consistent and remarkable experiential pattern that often unfolds when an individual is seemingly about to die."*
>
> —Kenneth Ring[1]

9

Near-Death Experiences

In 1981 George Gallup conducted a poll in which he surveyed 1,500 people who experienced a brush with death. He found that approximately one-third of these people admitted to having a "near-death experience." Extrapolating this ratio to include the entire population of the United States, Gallup estimated that as many as eight million people may have had a near-death experience.[2]

But what *is* a near-death experience? One person explained his experience this way:

> I was dying.
>
> I heard the doctor pronounce me dead. As I lay on the operating table of the large hospital, a loud, harsh buzzing began to reverberate in my head. At the same time, I sensed myself moving quickly through a long, dark tunnel. Then, suddenly, I found myself outside of my own physical body! Like a spectator, I watched the doctor's desperate attempts to revive my corpse.
>
> Soon, I saw the spirits of relatives and friends who had already died. I encountered a "being" of light. This being showed me an instant replay of my life and had me evaluate my past deeds.

Finally, I learned that my time to die had not yet come and that I had to return to my body. I resisted, for I had found my afterlife experience to be quite pleasant. Yet somehow, I was reunited with my physical body and lived.[3]

This person's experience is not unique. In fact, based on thousands of interviews with people who have gone through similar experiences, researchers say there are 15 characteristics that commonly occur in a near-death experience:

1. *Ineffability.* Most people say that no words can describe the near-death experience. What they went through is said to be inexpressible. Human language is insufficient to explain what occurred.

2. *Hearing the News.* Individuals typically say they heard themselves pronounced dead by medical personnel. To the doctors and nurses present, death seemed real because the heart or breathing had stopped and the person appeared to be physiologically dead. But the individual nevertheless claims to have heard him- or herself pronounced dead.

3. *Feelings of Peace and Quiet.* Most people who have had a near-death experience say they had sensations of extreme pleasure, peace, and quiet. It is these feelings that often motivate the individual to want to stay "dead" and not return to earthly life.

4. *The Noise.* During a near-death experience people often hear a noise. Sometimes the noise is pleasant, like rapturous music. In other (most) cases, the noise is harsh and disturbing, like a continuous buzzing or ringing sound.

5. *The Dark Tunnel.* A very common characteristic of the near-death experience is that people feel they are being jerked through a dark passageway or tunnel, often while hearing the noise described above.

6. *Out of the Body.* People typically say that they departed from their physical body and observed it laying on the operating table while doctors and nurses attempted resuscitation or pronounced death.

7. *Meeting Others.* It is often claimed that there are spiritual entities present to help the newly dead person through the experience. Sometimes these spiritual entities are loved ones who have already passed away.

8. *The Being of Light.* One of the most common characteristics of the near-death experience is encountering a being of light. Even though the light emanating from this being is brilliant, it does not hurt the eyes. This being also seems to emanate love and warmth. He communicates not with words but through thoughts. Often the communications deal with the meaning of life.

9. *The Review.* Sometimes individuals in a near-death experience witness a vivid review of their entire life. This life-review is said to provoke in them a recognition of the importance of loving other people. The review ends up helping them to understand the true meaning of life.

10. *The Border or Limit.* Individuals in a near-death experience often come upon an obstruction that prevents them from going any further in their journey or actually reaching the being of light. Sometimes this border is described as a fence, a door, or a body of water.

11. *Coming Back.* Because of the incredible feelings of peace and tranquillity, and because of the love and warmth emanating from the being of light, many individuals in a near-death experience want to stay in the presence of the being of light and not come back. They nevertheless return because they are told they haven't finished their tasks on earth. Other people say they felt obliged to return to earth

(without being asked) so they could complete unfinished tasks. The "return trip" is said to be instantaneous, back through the dark tunnel.

12. *Telling Others.* Most people who go through this experience say they are reticent about sharing the details with other people. They feel their experience is inexpressible. Moreover, they feel others will express skepticism upon hearing about what happened. Hence, most people choose to remain quiet.

13. *Effects on Lives.* It is claimed by many researchers that people who go through a near-death experience typically end up having more care and a more loving attitude toward other people. They also have a greater zeal for living and often feel they have a greater understanding of the meaning of life.

We should note, however, that other researchers have disputed this claim. These latter researchers say that many people who go through a near-death experience end up having severe psychological distress—so severe that they find it difficult to remain committed to relationships and hold down a vocation.

14. *New Views of Death.* Most people who go through a near-death experience say they no longer fear death. But neither do they seek it. They usually come to view death as a simple transition to another form of life. They do not fear any judgment or punishment in the next life.

15. *Corroboration.* A final characteristic of the near-death experience is that the individual is later able to corroborate specific events that would have been impossible for him or her to do unless he or she had been consciously observing things. Researcher Jerry Yamamoto explains, "Remarkably there are independent testimonies of people who have corroborated some

of the details in NDE [near-death experience] accounts; that is, specific incidents (e.g., in the hospital operating room) witnessed by those who were supposedly dead."[4]

It's essential for us to observe that not every person who has gone through a NDE reports the presence of all fifteen characteristics. In fact, most people experience just *some* of these characteristics. No two stories are identical. How many elements a person experiences seems to relate to how deep and how long he or she was apparently "dead."[5] It should also be noted that there are often variations in the order in which the 15 characteristics are experienced.

Who Is the Being of Light?

It has been claimed by numerous (not all) individuals who have had near-death experiences that the being of light they encountered was none other than Jesus Christ. As appealing as the idea may seem, this identification (at least in *most* cases) appears to be flawed because the so-called being of light typically says and does things contrary to the Christ of the Bible. Since Jesus is the same yesterday, today, and forever (Hebrews 13:8), it would be impossible for the being of light and Jesus to be one and the same. I believe that many of the people who go through near-death experiences actually encounter a *counterfeit* Christ.

The "Jesus" (being of light) typically encountered in near-death experiences teaches such things as:

- Death is good and is not to be feared;
- Sin is not a problem. In fact, "Jesus" often responds to human sin and shortcomings with humor;

- There is no hell to worry about;
- All people are welcome to heaven, regardless of whether a person has placed faith in Christ.
- All religions are equally valid.

Because these ideas clearly go against what the Jesus of the Bible taught, I think we have good reason to conclude that this "Jesus" is in fact a lying spirit (see John 8:44). We must remember that Satan has the ability to appear as an "angel of light" and his servants as "servants . . . of righteousness" (2 Corinthians 11:14-15). His goal, of course, is to lead people astray. He is happy to mimic a being of light if the end result is that he can lead people away from the true Christ of Scripture.

Consistent with those facts is the sad reality that many people who have had near-death experiences come out of the experience with a lower view of Scripture. One person concluded that "the Lord isn't interested in theology," and another said that God "didn't care about church doctrine at all."[6] The true Christ of Scripture, however, is most certainly interested in correct doctrine (*see* John 8:31-32).

Now, other individuals—particularly those who are affiliated with non-Christian religions—claim that the being of light was Buddha, or Krishna, or some other leader of a particular world religion.[7] Certainly this should raise "red flags" in the minds of Christians. Satan, the great counterfeiter, is seeking to keep people of all religions away from the true Christ of the Bible.

Betty Eadie's Experience:
Embraced by the Light

Near-death experiences have become a topic of mainstream interest in recent years due largely to Betty Eadie's blockbuster bestseller, *Embraced by the Light* (1992). This book is supposedly a firsthand report of Eadie's own near-death experience and events related to it. The book stayed on the *New York Times* bestseller list for over a year, selling more than a million copies.[8]

Eadie claims that in November 1973 she was "dead" for more than four hours. During this time, she claims her spirit was transported to heaven. While there, she was allegedly embraced by Jesus Christ and given a tour of heaven. She explains her initial experience (following "death") this way:

> I saw a pinpoint of light in the distance. . . . I was instinctively attracted to it. . . . As I approached it, I noticed the figure of a man standing in it, with the light radiating all around him. . . . I felt his light blending into mine, literally, and I felt my light being drawn to his. . . . And as our lights merged, I felt as if I had stepped into his countenance, and I felt an utter explosion of love. . . . I went to him and received his complete embrace and said over and over, "I'm home. I'm home. I'm finally home." I felt his enormous spirit and knew that I had always been a part of him, that in reality I had never been away from him. . . . There was no questioning who he was. I knew that he was my Savior, and friend, and God. He was Jesus Christ.[9]

Upon reading Eadie's book, a person comes away with the clear impression that there is nothing to fear in death. Indeed, as we pass through death's door, all of us enter into a glorious light. This "light" is brimming with unconditional love and acceptance for all people.[10]

Many people—including Christians—have read Eadie's account and have accepted it as gospel truth. A more discerning look at Eadie's book, however, reveals it to be full of spiritual error.

As a backdrop, we must remember that Scripture repeatedly warns us against spiritual impostors and counterfeits. Indeed, we are warned about false Christs (Matthew 24:5), false gospels (Galatians 1:6-9), and false teachings (Acts 20:28-31). For this reason we are called to "test the spirits to see whether they are from God" (1 John 4:1).[11]

In "testing" Eadie, we begin with the recognition that she is a Mormon, a fact that was veiled in the most widely distributed version of *Embraced by the Light.* Eadie originally marketed the book as a Mormon testimony in Mormon-dense parts of the country. She even included a one-page flyer, entitled "Of Special Interest to Members of the Church of Latter-day Saints," in which she spoke of her conversion to Mormonism.[12]

As we read through Eadie's book, we find descriptions of God, Jesus, and religion in general that blatantly contradict the biblical portrayal of these topics. Hence, whatever "Jesus" Eadie met during her near-death experience was certainly not the Jesus of the Bible.

For example, as my friend Doug Groothuis has noted in his excellent book *Deceived by the Light,* "When Jesus and 'the council of men' asked Eadie to return to earth, she apparently suffered from no sense of obligation to obey Christ. Instead, she protested and bartered with them. She consented to return only after she was told about her 'mission' on earth and after she *'made them* promise that the moment my mission was complete they would take me back home. . . . They agreed to *my terms.'* "[13] *This* Jesus is not the sovereign God of the universe who controls the affairs of humankind. He is just a member of a council who must negotiate terms with Eadie.

Eadie also speaks of Jesus more in terms of an advanced spirit-brother rather than a sovereign God. Her portrayal of

Jesus reflects Mormon teaching, which says that all of us (Jesus and *all* human beings) are spirit children of the heavenly father and mother, and all of us have the potential to become gods.

Sin is certainly not taken seriously in Eadie's book. In fact, during a "life-review" Eadie went through, Jesus allegedly "told her to lighten up on herself and not to take her acts of wrongdoing so seriously."[14]

Nowhere in her book does Eadie mention the need to repent of our sins against God (Psalm 51:4) or to place our faith in Christ for salvation (Acts 16:31). Instead, we are admonished to "look within" and "trust our abilities,"[15] particularly the inherent power of our thoughts.[16] (Does anyone smell New Age influence here?)

It is a fact that a weak view of sin always leads to a weak view of hell. And, as might be expected, Eadie omits any reference to hell in *Embraced by the Light*. Indeed, she says that all of us—even the worst of the human race—will eventually return to our heavenly home through Jesus. There will be no divine punishment.[17]

Eadie's view of God has definite pantheistic ("all is God") overtones. During her near-death experience she gazed upon a rose and "felt God in the plant, in me, his love pouring into us. We were all one."[18]

In keeping with this idea that "all is one," Eadie believes that all the different religions of the world should be accepted as appropriate for the people they serve. All roads are said to lead to God.[19]

To recap, then, Eadie would have us believe:

- there is no hell;
- there is no eternal punishment;
- heaven is the destiny of all people;

- we should therefore not fear death, nor fear God;
- we can all look forward to being "embraced by the light" at the moment of death.

What a stark contrast that is with biblical Christianity! In Scripture we find that there most definitely is a hell (Revelation 20:14); there will be eternal punishment (Matthew 25:46); heaven is not the destiny of all people but only of those who believe in Christ (John 14:1-3); unbelievers therefore *should* fear death and God (Luke 16:19-31).

Are Near-Death Experiences in the Bible?

There are some writers, such as near-death researcher Raymond Moody, who believe that near-death experiences can be found in the Bible. A representative example is Acts 9:3-6:

> As [Saul] neared Damascus on his journey, suddenly a light from heaven flashed around him. He fell to the ground and heard a voice say to him, "Saul, Saul, why do you persecute me?"
>
> "Who are you, Lord?" Saul asked.
>
> "I am Jesus, whom you are persecuting," he replied. "Now get up and go into the city, and you will be told what you must do."

Sometime later, after Saul had become a Christian (and his name was changed to Paul), he told King Agrippa about this same experience:

> "On one of these journeys I was going to Damascus with the authority and commission of the chief priests. About noon, O

king, as I was on the road, I saw a light from heaven, brighter than the sun, blazing around me and my companions. We all fell to the ground, and I heard a voice saying to me in Aramaic, 'Saul, Saul, why do you persecute me? . . .

"Then I asked, 'Who are you, Lord?'

" 'I am Jesus, whom you are persecuting,' the Lord replied. 'Now get up and stand on your feet. I have appeared to you to appoint you as a servant and as a witness. . . . I will rescue you from your own people and from the Gentiles. I am sending you to them to open their eyes and turn them from darkness to light, and from the power of Satan to God, so that they may receive forgiveness of sins and a place among those who are sanctified by faith in me' " (Acts 26:12-18).

As any careful reader can detect, there are serious problems with trying to argue that Paul had a near-death experience here. To begin, Paul was quite alive and was nowhere near death. By no stretch of the imagination, then, can this be called a near-death experience.

Second, notice that the light blinded Paul (Acts 9:8). In a typical near-death experience, the light is said to be brilliant but it is never so bright that it blinds anyone or hurts anyone's eyes.

Third, when he shared his testimony with King Agrippa, Paul never once mentioned anything remotely relating to a near-death experience. Everything was described by Paul in terms of something that happened to him on the road to Damascus.

Fourth, whereas most people tend to shy away from talking about their near-death experience, Paul spoke openly and with boldness about his encounter with the living Christ.

And finally, according to Acts 26:17-18, Jesus commissioned Paul to evangelize so that people may *receive forgiveness of sins by faith in Christ.* This is completely unlike the Jesus or the "being of light" in the typical near-death experience. Indeed, the Jesus of near-death experiences downplays sin and indicates that all people are welcome in heaven regardless of whether they've placed faith in Him.

We must conclude, then, that Acts 9 and 26 do not refer in any way to a near-death experience. To say that these chapters describe a near-death experience is to read something into the text that simply is not there.

What About "Hellish" Near-Death Experiences?

Dr. Charles Garfield, who has done extensive research on NDEs, said that "not everyone dies a blissful, accepting death. . . . Almost as many of the dying patients I interviewed reported negative visions (encounters with demonic figures and so forth) as reported blissful experiences, while some reported both."[20]

Dr. Maurice Rawlings wrote a book entitled *Beyond Death's Door,* which documents hellish NDEs. He said that about half of the NDEs he has researched were hellish in nature. But most people who experience such NDEs end up repressing the memory because it is so awful and traumatic.

In his book *Deceived by the Light,* Doug Groothuis recounts Dr. Rawlings's description of a particularly notable hellish near-death experience:

> While he was testing a man for a heart problem on a treadmill machine, the man went into cardiac arrest and began to turn blue. Rawlings immediately began external heart massage while a nurse administered mouth-to-mouth resuscitation. Other nurses brought in a breathing mask and pacemaker equipment.

The patient would occasionally regain consciousness but then lose it again whenever Rawlings would interrupt the compression of his chest in order to perform other life-saving procedures. Each time the man revived, he would scream, "I am in hell!" He would plead with Rawlings not to let him slip back into death, and would cry out repeatedly, "Don't stop!" This was unusual because CPR is a violent and painful procedure and many patients complain about the pain when they regain consciousness.

As Rawlings continued CPR, the man became increasingly alarmed and terrified. His pupils were dilating, and he was perspiring and trembling. Again he pleaded, "Don't you understand? I am in hell. Each time you quit [the CPR] I go back to hell! Don't let me go back to hell!" Rawlings wrote that "after three or four episodes of complete unconsciousness and clinical death from cessation of both heartbeat and breathing," the patient cried in desperation, "How do I stay out of hell?" Rawlings told the man what he remembered from Sunday school, and the man asked Rawlings to pray for him. Unusual as the context was, and although Rawlings was not a committed Christian at the time, he led the man in this prayer:

> Lord Jesus, I ask you to keep me out of hell.
> Forgive my sins.
> I turn my life over to you.
> If I die, I want to go to heaven.
> If I live, I'll be "on the hook" forever.

The man's condition stabilized, and he was taken to a hospital. A few days later, Rawlings questioned this man about his hell-like experience and found that he had forgotten it! Rawlings thinks that the experience had been so unnerving that it was repressed. Even so, the man became a committed Christian and a regular churchgoer after his experience of hell.[21]

Whatever we are to make of such an account, it is clear that this and other hellish near-death experiences call into question the claim by many people that individuals who enter the afterlife *always* have positive, tranquil, and peaceful experiences. Not everyone is "unconditionally accepted" by a loving being of light.

Explaining Near-Death Experiences

Researchers and experts have suggested a variety of explanations for what is going on in near-death experiences. Space limitations prohibit a detailed treatment of these theories. But here are some of the more popular ones:

1. Some experts say these experiences may result from a lack of oxygen to the brain. This is known as *hypoxia*. It is argued that this lack of oxygen to the brain accounts for sensations like going through a tunnel and seeing a bright light. The problem with this view, however, is that people who have gone through near-death experiences have not been found (in medical tests) to have less oxygen in their blood gases than other people.

2. Some experts have suggested that going through a dark tunnel and then seeing a bright light are actually deeply embedded memories of the birth experience. Astronomer and scientist Carl Sagan holds to this view. Critics respond by saying that a memory of birth would be traumatic, not pleasant (like some near-death experiences). Furthermore, during the birth experience the baby's face is pressed against the birth canal, which is much different than the feeling of going rapidly through a dark tunnel. As well, it is argued that the baby's brain is not developed enough to retain such memories.

3. Other suggested explanations include trauma or injury to the brain, severe psychological stress that may cause the release of chemicals in the brain that could induce certain experiences, or perhaps hallucinations caused by various medications.

As researchers John Weldon and John Ankerberg point out, however, such alternative theories do not really explain the various details of the typical near-death experience. For example, these theories "cannot explain how people who were brain dead at the time are later able to describe in vivid detail the attempts of medical personnel to resuscitate them."[22] Could it be that many of these experiences are actually caused by the evil one—Satan, the father of lies, who has the ability to perform counterfeit miracles (2 Thessalonians 2:9)?

The Connection with Occultism

Many researchers have noted a clear connection between near-death experiences and occultism. Weldon and Ankerberg, for example, tell us that "in large measure the NDE [near-death experience] is merely one form of the occult out-of-body experience (OBE)."[23] Moreover, "both the NDE and OBE have many other similarities including . . . spiritistic contacts, world view changes, and development of psychic powers."[24]

In keeping with Weldon and Ankerberg's findings, near-death researcher Kenneth Ring commented that "I could not help noticing the frequency with which psychic events were spontaneously reported by NDErs and how often these experiences were said to have occurred following the NDE. . . . Many NDErs simply claimed that their psychic sensitivities have developed strikingly since their NDE."[25]

What kinds of psychic phenomena are we talking about? Some people experience astral travel or out-of-body experiences (that is, the soul leaves the body and travels around the so-called astral realm). Some people develop clairvoyance (the ability to perceive things that are outside the natural range of human senses). Some people develop telepathic abilities (which involves mystical communication via thoughts alone). And many people come into contact with spirit guides, who allegedly stay with the person for the rest of his or her life.

Now, here's an important point: Occultism and psychic phenomena are utterly condemned by God in Scripture. Anyone who doubts that should meditate on Deuteronomy 18:10-13. It is clear, then, that much of what is going on in so-called near-death experiences is in fact not of God. *Reader beware!*

A Key Consideration: These Are Not Actual Deaths

We must keep in mind that near-death experiences do not actually prove anything about the final state of the dead. After all, these experiences are *near-death* experiences, not *once-for-all completely dead* experiences. In fact, as one writer said, near-death experiences "may tell us no more about death than someone who has been near Denver but never within city limits can tell us about that town. Both NDEs (near-Denver and near-death experiences) are bereft of certitude. . . . In both cases, more reliable maps are available."[26]

The map for near-death experiences is, of course, the Bible. Scripture defines death as the separation of the spirit from the body (James 2:26). And true death occurs *only once* (*see* Hebrews 9:27).

But Satan, the father of lies, wants us to believe that near-death experiences give us a sure indication of what our final state will be in death. He does this to deceive people. Christian pastor Douglas Connelly thus warns:

> I am convinced that much of what we hear regarding such encounters is our enemy's deliberate attempt to deceive people about what really lies beyond death's door. The prospect of death and of personal accountability to God has often moved people to seriously consider the claims of Christ and their own destinies. If people believe, however, based on a few near-death encounters, that death will lead them to a place of warmth and love and acceptance regardless of their relationship to Christ, they will no longer be moved to evaluate their lives.[27]

Kenneth Ring said that "one of the most consistent findings to emerge from the body of near-death research is that people who have had NDEs do not as a rule fear death at all; furthermore, their loss of the fear of death appears to be permanent following an NDE."[28]

Since these people conclude from their experience that they will live forever in a heavenly environment with no consequences for sin, they see no need to trust in a Savior. Satan and his horde of demons must jump for joy every time someone draws this conclusion.

What Can We Conclude?

As we have seen in this chapter, many accounts of near-death experiences have clear connections with occultism and must be outright rejected. As well, many of the accounts—such as

Betty Eadie's—portray a "Jesus" doing and saying things that go against the biblical Jesus. These too must be outright rejected. Does this mean we must conclude that every single person's experience is with a counterfeit Christ and holds no truth to it?

In his discerning article on near-death experiences in the *Christian Research Journal,* researcher Jerry Yamamoto wisely suggested that since near-death experiences "are of a subjective nature, determining their source is largely a speculative venture. With divine, demonic, and several natural factors all meriting considerations, a single, universal explanation for NDEs becomes quite risky."[29]

Some Christian researchers suggest that while we must be extremely cautious on this issue, it is possible that *some* people may have had bona fide near-death experiences with Jesus Christ. This group would especially include Christians, as well as people who became Christians as a direct result of their encounter.

As Jerry Yamamoto said, "If the message and experience of an NDE does not distort or conflict with biblical teachings, then we should be careful not to speak against that which resulted in salvation and may have been a genuine work of God."[30] Yamamoto cites a case where he thinks this is in fact what occurred. (A man named Dan became a devout Christian immediately after his near-death experience.[31])

Bible scholars Gary R. Habermas and J.P. Moreland, after an extensive study, concluded that "just as you can't have fake money without real money, so you can't have fake NDEs without real ones. You can't counterfeit what doesn't exist."[32] Their point is that even though there are many, many counterfeit near-death experiences that portray a counterfeit Jesus who preaches a counterfeit message, so also are there some genuine near-death experiences in which people may have actually encountered Jesus Christ.

My advice is this: No matter what kind of experience you have, always test it against Scripture (*see* 1 Thessalonians 5:21). If *anything* contradicts the Word of God in any way, it must be rejected. *Make the Scriptures your sole measuring stick.* God's Word will keep you on track.

Keeping Things in Perspective

As we carefully ponder the pages of Scripture, we can arrive at a proper perspective toward other-worldly experiences. In 2 Corinthians 12 we read that Paul was "caught up to the third heaven" (verse 2) and was "caught up to paradise" (verse 3). While there he "heard inexpressible things, things that man is not permitted to tell" (verse 4). And to keep him from "becoming conceited because of these surpassingly great revelations," there was given him a thorn in the flesh (verse 7).

Here's the key point: As we examine the rest of Paul's writings, it becomes abundantly clear that his otherworld vision was just a minor footnote to his faith. He didn't talk about it much. Rather, he based his faith in the afterlife solely on the resurrection of Jesus Christ: "If Christ has not been raised, your faith is futile; you are still in your sins. Then those also who have fallen asleep in Christ are lost" (1 Corinthians 15:17-18).

Let us resolve to be careful . . . and follow Paul's example.

"There is only one being who can satisfy the last aching abyss of the human heart, and that is the Lord Jesus Christ."

—Oswald Chambers (1874-1917)[1]

10

Helping Those Who Grieve

I RECENTLY CAME across the following account of a man in deep grief. His story powerfully reflects what each of us go through when a loved one dies. Reflect on his words:

> The rays of a late morning South Carolina sun struck me full on the face as I stepped through the door of the hospital. The squint of my eyes, however, was not occasioned by the rays of the sun; it was the visible display of the anguish and despair that wracked my very life.

> I had spent several hours with my sobbing wife. Now I was about to keep the appointment that would prove to be the emotional climax of the day my world collapsed.

> On my way to the appointment, I stopped at a diner to have a cup of coffee and to bolster my courage. I was oblivious to everything except the appointment that awaited me.

> Leaving the diner, I made my way to a large white house, located on a corner in Columbia, South Carolina. I followed the owner into a large room, where he soon left me alone. I slowly made my way across a thick rug on the floor to a table on the far side of the room.

Upon the table was a white box. I stood before that white box for endless eternities before I finally summoned enough courage to look over the top and down into the white box, at the lifeless body of my son.

At that sight my world collapsed. I would have given up all of my academic and athletic awards. I would have given up the prestigious executive training program I was engaged in with one of the largest international oil companies. I would have given anything. For the first time in my life, I had come to a hurdle I could not clear. My world collapsed.[2]

Christians Are Not Immune to Grief

Christians are not immune to the pain of grief. Even though Christ has taken the "sting" out of death (1 Corinthians 15:55), it is nevertheless extremely painful when a family member or friend dies. Even the great apostle Paul considered death an "enemy" yet to be conquered (1 Corinthians 15:26).

In Western society many young boys are told from early childhood, "Big boys don't cry." As they reach their teenage years, they are told, "Men don't cry." Upon life's misfortunes they are told, "Take it like a man." Such unfortunate comments fail to recognize that weeping is the language of the soul—and that weeping is *the* proper response to grief.

Some Christians have wrongly surmised that a "true" Christian who has faith in God should not grieve over the loss of a loved one. But this is a gross distortion of what the Scriptures teach. We must recognize that the Bible clearly distinguishes between people who "grieve" and people who "grieve like the rest of men, who have no hope" (1 Thessalonians 4:13).

Do you remember the story of Lazarus's death in Bethany? Lazarus was a close friend of Jesus. After Lazarus died, Jesus went to Bethany to be with Lazarus's family. We read in John 11:35 that upon witnessing the scene in Bethany, "Jesus wept." He was so deeply moved that He cried over His friend's passing. And the Jews who witnessed this said, "See how he loved him!" (verse 36).

It is natural and right for us to be sad—to ache and grieve and cry when a loved one dies. When Stephen was put to death, "godly men buried [him] and mourned deeply for him" (Acts 8:2). *Godly Christians can mourn deeply.*

Understanding Bereavement

Christians who have the hope of eternal life can be confident that they will spend eternity with their Christian loved ones. That is an incredible source of strength and comfort. Even so, this hope does not eliminate the pain and grief of the present moment.

When Pastor Rick Taylor's young son Kyle died, there came a time when he spoke these touching words from his heart: "Kyle is dead. He is gone. I will never see my precious son grow up. I will never throw the football with him again. I will never again help him learn how to grip a bat or clap for joy because he hit a ball. I will never again sit by his side and read to him at bedtime. I will never again go for walks with him and hear him growing up as he talks with me. I will never see the man he would have become."[3]

The same kinds of feelings are present when a spouse dies. "The day-to-day reality faced by the widow is that she will never again be held by her husband in this life. They will never again hold hands as they take strolls under autumn skies. They will never again joke and laugh or hurt and cry together. They will never again watch the sunset together. They will never again lie beside each other in bed and talk together and love together."⁴

This is the pain of bereavement. It is not just the fact that someone has died. It is the fact that in this world we will never again do the most precious and dear things with the person who has died. It is a hurt that wounds the heart like no other hurt.

Grief and Feelings of Isolation

We must remember that the bereaved often feel isolated and cut off from other people—especially in the weeks following the funeral of their loved one. At the funeral there is typically a great outpouring of love. And that is as it should be. But then friends and relatives plow back into their lives, often forgetting the pain that the bereaved continues to go through in the weeks and months that follow. We should make every effort to stay in regular contact during these difficult months.

We should be especially sensitive to the bereaved's feelings of awkwardness, unconnectedness, and even of being stigmatized after the loss of their loved one. Following the death of his wife, C.S. Lewis kept of diary of his daily grief and published it in a book called *A Grief Observed*. In it he spoke of the awkwardness he felt in the presence of other people following his wife's death:

> An odd byproduct of my loss is that I'm aware of being an embarrassment to everyone I meet. At work, at the club, in the street, I see people, as they approach me, trying to make up their minds whether they'll "say something about it" or not. I hate it if they do, and if they don't. . . . R. has been avoiding me for a week. I like best the well-brought-up

young men, almost boys, who walk up to me as if I were a dentist, turn very red, get it over, and then edge away to the bar as quickly as they decently can. Perhaps the bereaved ought to be isolated in special settlements like lepers.[5]

Lewis's words are a call for us to genuinely *be there* for people who grieve. First and foremost, we can be there for our grieving friend or family member by regularly lifting him or her up in prayer before God. Pray for his or her emotional stability, physical health, spiritual life, and eternal perspective. Ask God for His guidance in how you can be of help.

Being there also includes recognizing that everyone faces death in their own way, and not necessarily as we would or think they should. We must be sensitive to discern when our company and spoken support are needed, or when our quiet presence and a listening ear would be more appreciated. The bottom line of being there is to be sensitive, thoughtful, and understanding.

Grief Must Be Expressed

Grief must be expressed in some way. It is much like the steam in a steam engine. Unless it can escape in a controlled way, the pressure will steadily build up and the boiler will explode. Unless we learn to express grief, we can look forward to an emotional and psychological explosion of some sort. Emotional release is a must.

Hence, when you are helping someone who is going through grief, be aware that his or her grief must be expressed. Be available as a sounding board. And don't be afraid to cry along with your grieving friend.

The grieving process typically manifests itself by such symptoms as crying, difficulty in sleeping, and a loss of appetite. You also need to be aware of the wide variety of emotions the bereaved person may experience. Some people may feel aggrieved at being "deserted" by their departed loved one or angry at God. Sometimes there is guilt—perhaps over a harsh word spoken, a withheld blessing, the neglected "shoulds" of a lifetime of living together, or even because the final illness wasn't taken more seriously.

Later, the grief may turn to deep depression—sometimes even despondency. This is especially the case when friends and family have gone on with their lives and are no longer offering the emotional and spiritual support they did at first. Loneliness may become acute. Help your friend unravel his or her raging sea of emotions. You may even discern the need to direct him or her to receive counsel from his or her pastor.

The Ministry of Comfort

One of the reasons you and I can minister to other people who are grieving is that we ourselves have gone through grief in our own lives. There have been times when we have grieved at the loss of a loved one and have experienced God's great comfort. And now we can be used by God to bring comfort to others.

As the apostle Paul said in 2 Corinthians 1:3-4, "Praise be to the God and Father of our Lord Jesus Christ, the Father of compassion and the God of all comfort, who comforts us in all our troubles, so that we can comfort those in any trouble with the comfort we ourselves have received from God." Seen in this light, you and I can become a channel of blessing through which God's comfort can flow to the person who hurts.

The Lord Is Our Refuge

Sometimes when a loved one dies, the person closest to the deceased asks, "Where is God's love and plan in this?" Help the grieving person to see that although we may not know God's sovereign plan, we *can* take refuge in the fact that we know the Planner. For the Planner—Jesus Christ Himself—knows the meaning of grief. He wept at the funeral of His friend Lazarus. He suffered as all of us suffer when someone dies. And most important, He cares deeply for each one of us. He cares more than we know.

The Scriptures tell us that "the LORD is close to the broken-hearted and saves those who are crushed in spirit" (Psalm 34:18). Truly it is the Lord who is our refuge when a loved one dies. He Himself is our balm. And He often brings His comfort to us through the pages of Scripture. Bible verses you may want to share with your grieving friend or family member include Deuteronomy 31:8, Psalm 46:1, Psalm 62:2, John 6:51, John 11:25, 2 Corinthians 4:17-18, and Hebrews 4:16.

Going on with Life

After time passes by—during which months of grief seem to have overshadowed everything—eventually there comes a point when life isn't so painful. In *Grief and How to Live with It,* Sharan Morris says, "Finally, a remarkable thing begins to happen. You notice that for short periods the hurt is not so great. This is the beginning of your healing."[6] The Lord will sustain a person not only through his or her initial grief, but He will also help that person become whole again. *He is faithful.*

A key goal in ministering to people who grieve is to help them gain an eternal perspective that will enable them to move beyond their grief and get on with their life. Consider these words from a father who gave some important counsel to his daughter on the first anniversary of her mother's death.

"I had forty wonderful years with your Mom," he said, "the best years of my life. But that part of my life is over. Finished!"

"But Dad . . ."

"No buts, listen to me."

His clear blue eyes stared intensely into mine. I couldn't turn away from him, as much as I wanted to.

"They were the best years of my life," he repeated. "Your mother is no longer with me; this truth has to be faced. But I am alive and must live the time allotted me until she and I are together again."

His voice trembled, but it was not uncertain.

"She is gone," he said, "but no one can take away the wonderful memories. They are part of me, the happy memories and the sad ones. But only a part. I can't let them possess me or I couldn't get through my days. Every day is a gift from God. It must be lived with joy. It is just a taste of the joy to come when we will all be together again."

I kissed him then, not realizing that our conversation would one day be one of my fondest memories. Recalling that day has always been a great strength to me, particularly today— the first anniversary of my dear father's death.'

How completely satisfying to turn from our limitations to a God who has none. Eternal years lie in His heart. For Him time does not pass, it remains; and those who are in Christ share with Him all the riches of limitless time and endless years.

— A.W. Tozer (1897-1963)[1]

11

Looking Toward Eternity

THE INCREDIBLE GLORY of the afterlife should motivate each of us to live faithfully during our relatively short time on earth. Especially when difficult times come, we must remember that we are but pilgrims on our way to another land—to the undiscovered country, the final frontier of heaven where God Himself dwells.

J.I. Packer once said that the "lack of long, strong thinking about our promised hope of glory is a major cause of our plodding, lack-luster lifestyle."[2] Packer points to the Puritans as a much-needed example for us, for they believed that "it is the heavenly Christian that is the lively Christian."[3] The Puritans understood that we "run so slowly, and strive so lazily, because we so little mind the prize. . . . So let Christians animate themselves daily to run the race set before them by practicing heavenly meditation."[4]

How I have come to appreciate the Puritans! How I personally seek to imitate their example! The Puritans "saw themselves as God's pilgrims, traveling home through rough country; God's warriors, battling the world, the flesh, and the devil; and God's servants, under orders to worship, fellowship, and do all the good they could as they went along."[5] We should have the same attitude.

I am particularly impressed with the writings of Puritan Richard Baxter. Truly he had some habits worthy of imitation. His first habit was to "estimate everything—values, priorities, possessions, relationships, claims, tasks—as these things will appear when one actually comes to die."[6] In other words, he weighed everything in terms of eternal benefit. After all, our life on earth is short; our life in heaven is forever. If we work only for the things of this earth, what eternal benefit will all of it have?

Baxter's second habit was to "dwell on the glory of the heavenly life to which one was going."[7] Baxter daily practiced "holding heaven at the forefront of his thoughts and desires."[8] The hope of heaven brought him joy, and joy brought him strength. Baxter once said, "A heavenly mind is a joyful mind; this is the nearest and truest way to live a life of comfort. . . . A heart in heaven will be a most excellent preservative against temptations, a powerful means to kill thy corruptions."[9]

A "Top-Down" Perspective

Gary R. Habermas and J.P. Moreland have come up with a term I like a lot: the *"top-down" perspective*. That's precisely what we need during our earthly pilgrimage as we sojourn toward the heavenly country:

> The God of the universe invites us to view life and death from His eternal vantage point. And if we do, we will see how readily it can revolutionize our lives: daily anxieties, emotional hurts, tragedies, our responses and responsibilities to others, possessions, wealth, and even physical pain and death. All of this and much more can be informed and

influenced by the truths of heaven. The repeated witness of the New Testament is that believers should view all problems, indeed, their entire existence, from what we call the "top-down" perspective: God and His kingdom first, followed by various aspects of our earthly existence.[10]

A key Bible passage that supports the top-down perspective is Matthew 6:19-34. Here, Jesus informs us that anxiety will not change anything. Certainly it will not increase the length of our lives (*see* verse 27). Our goal therefore should be to store up treasures in heaven. This will help rid our lives of anxiety. Make note of this principle: *Our hearts will coincide with the placement of our treasures.*

If we are usually anxious over temporal problems, our hearts are not centered on what should be our first love. If we have perpetual anxiety, we are more occupied with transient realities than Jesus intended. So in Matthew 6:19-34 we have a ready-made test by which we can assess the depth of our beliefs.[11]

Our goal, then, should be to maintain a top-down perspective. This perspective is a radical love of God that places Him first and foremost in every aspect of our lives. "Set your minds on things above, not on earthly things" (Colossians 3:2). And when we do this, God has promised to meet all our earthly needs as part of the package (Matthew 6:33)! What could be better?

Hope that Fuels Faith

Our *hope* in the future glory of the afterlife fuels our *faith* in the present. Hope and faith—these are closely tied to each other in the pages of Scripture. The apostle Paul tells us that faith involves "being sure of what we hope for" (Hebrews 11:1).

In his classic *Institutes of the Christian Religion,* John Calvin delineates for us how hope relates to faith: "Hope refreshes faith, that it may not become weary. It sustains faith to the final goal, that it may not fail in midcourse, or even at the starting gate. In short, by unremitting renewing and restoring, it invigorates faith again and again with perseverance."[12]

One of my favorite Old Testament characters is Moses. His life vividly illustrates how hope can feed and sustain faith:

> *By faith* Moses, when he had grown up, refused to be known as the son of Pharaoh's daughter. He chose to be mistreated along with the people of God rather than to enjoy the pleasures of sin for a short time. He regarded disgrace for the sake of Christ as of greater value than the treasures of Egypt, *because he was looking ahead to his reward. By faith* he left Egypt, not fearing the king's anger; he persevered because *he saw him who is invisible.*" (Hebrews 11:24-27, emphasis added).

Moses could have had immeasurable power, authority, and riches if he had chosen to stay in Egypt. Yet he gave it all up because of his faith in God. He perceived another King, another kingdom. And his faith was nourished by his hope of a future reward, a hope of living in the eternal city with the living Lord of the universe, a hope that gave him an eternal perspective.

Truly our faith enables us to perceive the eternal. I very much like the way John Wesley put it: "True Christian faith fulfills man's desires to perceive the eternal. It gives him a more extensive knowledge of all things invisible. Living faith introduces him to what the eye has not seen, nor the ear heard, nor the heart conceived in the clearest light, with the fullest certainty and evidence. Knowing these benefits, who would not wish for such a faith? With faith comes not only this awareness, but also the fulfillment of the promise of holiness and happiness."[13]

So, then, walking by sight we behold disease, decay, and death as regular features of our world. But walking by faith enables us to see the reality beyond the physical senses into the world of the eternal. And as we have seen throughout this book, the destiny of those who believe in Jesus Christ is a wonderful one indeed. For we will live forever with Christ in resurrected bodies that will never again be susceptible to disease, decay, and death. *Let our faith cause us to rejoice in this!*

The great preacher Charles Spurgeon once said, "A little faith will bring your soul to heaven; a great faith will bring heaven to your soul."[14] One of the ways that faith brings heaven to our souls relates to the realization of a heavenly destiny with Christ. Such faith rests in the assurance that regardless of what happens on this puny speck of a planet, our destiny is the eternal city, the heavenly country, at the very side of Christ.

Death Holds No Fear, For It Is Conquered

Because of our personal relationship with the Lord, we no longer need to fear death; it has been conquered. As the psalmist said, "Even though I walk through the valley of the shadow of death, I will fear no evil, for you are with me; your rod and your staff, they comfort me" (Psalm 23:4).

And when believers pass through death's door, neither pain nor death will ever be faced by them again, for God "will wipe every tear from their eyes. There will be no more death or mourning or crying or pain, for the old order of things has passed away" (Revelation 21:4).

Hermann Lange's life perfectly illustrates what it means to live without the fear of death. Lange was a young German preacher who stood among the Christians who spoke out against Adolf Hitler's repression of the gospel. Like many others, Lange was arrested, interrogated. tried as a criminal, and condemned to die before a firing squad. On the last day of his life he wrote a farewell letter to his parents:

> When this letter comes to your hands, I shall no longer be among the living. The thing that has occupied our thoughts constantly for many months, never leaving them free, is now about to happen.
>
> If you ask me what state I am in, I can only answer: I am, first, in a joyous mood, and second, filled with great antici-pation. As regards the first feeling, today means the end of all suffering and all earthly sorrow for me—and "God will wipe away every tear" from my eyes. What consolation, what mar-velous strength emanates from faith in Christ, who has pre-ceded us in death. In Him, I have put my faith, and precisely today I have faith in Him more firmly than ever. . . .
>
> And as to the second feeling [of anticipation], this day brings the greatest hour of my life! Everything that till now I have done, struggled for, and accomplished has at bottom been di-rected to this one goal, whose barrier I shall penetrate today. "Eye hath not seen, nor ear heard, neither have entered into the heart of man, the things which God hath prepared for them that love him" (1 Corinthians 2:9). . . .
>
> Until we meet again above in the presence of the Father of Light,
>
> Your joyful Hermann[15]

> *"He who created us without our help will not save us without our consent."*
>
> —Saint Augustine of Hippo (354-430)[1]

Postscript:
An Invitation to Believe

Do you have a personal relationship with Jesus Christ? Most of you probably do. But perhaps some of you do not. And perhaps you—after reading in this book about the joys of spending eternity with Jesus in heaven—are now desirous of that relationship. It is for you that I have written this final chapter.

You see, a personal relationship with Jesus is the most important decision you could ever make in your life. It is unlike any other relationship. For if you go into eternity without this relationship, you will spend eternity apart from Him.

So, if you will allow me, I'd like to tell you how you can come to know Jesus personally.

First you need to recognize that . . .

God *Desires* a Personal Relationship with You

God created you (Genesis 1:27). And He didn't just create you to exist all alone and apart from Him. He created you with the desire to have a personal relationship with you.

Remember, God had face-to-face encounters and fellowship with Adam and Eve, the first couple (Genesis 3:8-19). And just as God fellowshiped with them, so also does He desire to fellowship *with you* (1 Corinthians 1:9). God *loves* you (John 3:16). Never forget that fact.

The problem is . . .

Humanity's Sin Problem Blocks a Relationship with God

When Adam and Eve chose to sin against God in the Garden of Eden, they catapulted the entire human race—to which they gave birth—into sin. Since the time of Adam and Eve, every human being has been born into the world with a propensity to sin.

The apostle Paul affirmed that "sin entered the world through one man, and death through sin" (Romans 5:12). Indeed, we are told that "through the disobedience of the one man the many were made sinners" (Romans 5:19). Ultimately this means that "death came through a man. . . . in Adam all die" (1 Corinthians 15:21-22).

Jesus often spoke of sin in metaphors that illustrate the havoc it can wreak in our lives. He described sin as blindness (Matthew 23:16-26), sickness (Matthew 9:12), being enslaved in bondage (John 8:34), and living in darkness (John 8:12; 12:35-46). Moreover, Jesus taught that sin is a universal condition and that all people are guilty before God (Romans 3:10-11).

Jesus also said that both inner thoughts and external acts render a person guilty (Matthew 5:28). He taught that from within the human heart come evil thoughts, sexual immorality, theft, murder, adultery, greed, malice, deceit, envy, slander, arrogance, and folly (Mark 7:21-23). Moreover, He affirmed that God is fully aware of every person's sins—both external acts and inner thoughts; nothing escapes His notice (Matthew 22:18; Luke 6:8; John 4:17-19).

Of course, some people are more morally upright than others. But we *all* fall short of God's infinite standards (Romans 3:23). In a contest to see who can throw a rock to the moon, I am sure a muscular athlete would be able to throw the rock much further than I could. But ultimately, all human beings would fall short of the task. Similarly, all of us fall short of measuring up to God's perfect holy standards.

Though the sin problem is a serious one, God has graciously provided a solution:

Jesus Died for Our Sins and Made Salvation Possible

God's absolute holiness demands that sin be punished. The good news of the gospel, however, is that Jesus has taken this punishment on Himself. God loves us so much that He sent Jesus to bear the penalty for our sins!

Jesus affirmed that it was for the very purpose of dying that He came into the world (John 12:27). Moreover, He perceived His death as being a sacrificial offering *for the sins of humanity* (Matthew 26:26-28). Jesus took His sacrificial mission with utmost seriousness, for He knew that without Him, humanity would certainly perish (Matthew 16:25; John 3:16) and spend eternity apart from God in a place of great suffering (Matthew 10:28; 25:41; Luke 16:22-28).

Jesus therefore described His mission this way: "The Son of Man did not come to be served, but to serve, and to give his life as a ransom for many" (Matthew 20:28). "The Son of Man came to seek and to save what was lost" (Luke 19:10), for "God did not send his Son into the world to condemn the world, but to save the world through him" (John 3:17).

However, the benefits of Christ's death on the cross are not automatically applied to your life. God requires you to . . .

Believe in Jesus Christ

By His sacrificial death on the cross, Jesus took the sins of the entire world on Himself and made salvation available for everyone (1 John 2:2). But this salvation is not automatic. Only those who personally choose to believe in Christ are saved. This is the consistent testimony of the Jesus in the Bible. Consider His words:

- "God so loved the world that he gave his one and only Son, that whoever *believes* in him shall not perish but have eternal life" (John 3:16).
- "My Father's will is that everyone who looks to the Son and *believes* in him shall have eternal life, and I will raise him up at the last day" (John 6:40).
- "I am the resurrection and the life. He who *believes* in me will live, even though he dies" (John 11:25).

Choosing *not* to believe in Jesus, by contrast, leads to eternal condemnation: "Whoever *believes* in him is not condemned, but whoever *does not believe* stands condemned already because he has not believed in the name of God's one and only Son" (John 3:18, emphasis added).

Free at Last: Forgiven of All Sins

When you believe in Christ the Savior, a wonderful thing happens. God forgives you of all your sins. *All of them!* He puts them completely out of His sight. Ponder for a few minutes the following verses, which speak of the forgiveness of those who have believed in Christ:

- "In him we have redemption through his blood, the forgiveness of sins, in accordance with the riches of God's grace" (Ephesians 1:7).
- God said, "Their sins and lawless acts I will remember no more" (Hebrews 10:17-18).
- "Blessed is he whose transgressions are forgiven, whose sins are covered. Blessed is the man whose sin the LORD does not count against him and in whose spirit is no deceit" (Psalm 32:1-2).
- "For as high as the heavens are above the earth, so great is his love for those who fear him; as far as the east is from the west, so far has he removed our transgressions from us" (Psalm 103:11-12).

Such forgiveness is wonderful indeed, for none of us can possibly work our way into heaven or be good enough to warrant God's good favor. Because of what Jesus has done for us, we can freely receive the gift of salvation. It is a gift provided solely through the grace of God (Ephesians 2:8-9). And all of it is ours by simply believing in Jesus.

Don't Put It Off

It is highly dangerous to put off turning to Christ for salvation, for you do not know the day of your death. What if it happens this evening? "Death is the destiny of every man; the living should take this to heart" (Ecclesiastes 7:2).

If God is speaking to your heart now, then *now* is your door of opportunity to believe. "Seek the LORD while he may be found; call on him while he is near" (Isaiah 55:6).

Follow Along in Prayer

Would you like to place your faith in Jesus for the forgiveness of your sins and guarantee your place in heaven alongside Him for all eternity? If so, pray the following prayer.

Keep in mind that it's not the prayer itself that saves you. It is the *faith in your heart* that saves you. So, let this prayer be a simple expression of the faith that is in your heart:

Dear Jesus:
I want to have a relationship with You.
I know I can't save myself, because I know I'm a sinner.
Thank You for dying on the cross on my behalf.
I believe You died *for me,* and I accept Your free gift of salvation.
Thank You, Jesus.
Amen.

Welcome to God's Forever Family

On the authority of the Word of God, I can now assure you that you are a part of God's forever family. If you prayed the above prayer with a heart of faith, you will spend all eternity by the side of Jesus in heaven. Welcome to God's family!

If you've just become a Christian, I want to help you. I'd like to send you some free materials that will help you grow in your faith.

If you're already a Christian, I'd like to hear from you, too. At Reasoning from the Scriptures Ministries, we have many resources that will help you mature as a Christian.

Please write:

Ron Rhodes
Reasoning from the Scriptures Ministries
P.O. Box 80087
Rancho Santa Margarita, CA 92688

God bless you!

Appendix:
What About Suicide?

I AM SOMETIMES asked what the Bible says about suicide. Because suicide is a growing problem in our society, I want to briefly address what the Scriptures say about it.

Let's begin with the recognition that, from a biblical perspective, the issues of life and death are in the sovereign hands of God alone. Job said to God, "Man's days are determined; you [O God] have decreed the number of his months and have set limits he cannot exceed" (Job 14:5). David said to God, "All the days ordained for me were written in your book before one of them came to be" (Psalm 139:16).

Moreover, suicide goes against the commandments of God. In fact, the sixth commandment tells us, "You shall not murder" (Exodus 20:13). This command is based on the sanctity of human life. We must remember that man was created in the image of God (Genesis 1:27).

It is important to understand that the command, "You shall not murder" has no direct object. That is, it doesn't say, "You shall not murder someone else" or, "You shall not murder your fellow man." It simply says, "You shall not murder." The prohibition thus includes not just the murder of one's fellow man but even the murder of oneself.[1] While suicide is certainly not the "unforgivable sin,"* we must never forget that God prohibits murder of any kind.

Christian pastors and counselors often point out that a believer who ends his life also forever ends his opportunities to witness and serve the Lord on earth. Furthermore, suicide is one of the greatest acts of selfishness, for in it the individual caters to his own desires and his own will, ignoring the catastrophic effects it has on other people.

The lives of some of the saints in the Bible are instructive on the issue of suicide. There were times when certain servants of God were so severely tested and distressed that they wished for their own death (*see* 1 Kings 19:4; Jonah 4:8). But these individuals did not take matters into their own hands and kill themselves. Instead, they let God rescue them. We can learn a lesson here. When we are filled with despair, we must turn to God and not commit suicide. *God will see us through.*

The apostle Paul certainly went through tough times. In 2 Corinthians 1:8 we read about the severity of his distress: "We do not want you to be uninformed, brothers, about the hardships we suffered in the province of Asia. We were under great pressure, far beyond our ability to endure, so that *we despaired even of life*" (emphasis added).

Nevertheless, Paul did not succumb to breaking God's commandment against murder and commit suicide. He depended on God, and the Lord came through and gave Paul all the sustenance he needed to make it through his ordeal.

Following Paul's example, we too must depend on God when life gets rough. And just as God sustained Paul through his difficulties, so also will He sustain us.

---

*Some sensitive Christians have wondered if committing suicide causes a person to lose his or her salvation, leading to an eternity in hell. There is no scriptural justification for such a harsh view. The Bible says that people who have trusted in Christ are *saved forever* and will never lose their salvation (*see* Romans 8:30; Ephesians 4:30).

Bibliography

Abanes, Richard. *Embraced by the Light and the Bible*. Camp Hill, PA: Horizon Books, 1994.

Ankerberg, John, and Weldon, John. *The Facts on Life After Death*. Eugene, OR: Harvest House Publishers, 1992.

Berkhof, Louis. *Manual of Christian Doctrine*. Grand Rapids, MI: William B. Eerdmans, 1983.

Blanchard, John. *Whatever Happened to Hell?* Durham, England: Evangelical Press, 1993.

Calvin, John. *Institutes of the Christian Religion*. Philadelphia, PA: Westminster, 1960.

Chafer, Lewis Sperry, and Walvoord, John F. *Major Bible Themes*. Grand Rapids, MI: Zondervan Publishing House, 1975.

Connelly, Douglas. *What the Bible Really Says: After Life*. Downers Grove, IL: InterVarsity Press, 1995.

Eadie, Betty. *Embraced by the Light*. Placerville, CA: Gold Leaf Press, 1992.

Elwell, Walter A., ed. *Topical Analysis of the Bible*. Grand Rapids, MI: Baker Book House, 1991,

Erickson, Millard J. *Christian Theology*. Grand Rapids, MI: Baker Book House, 1985.

Groothuis, Doug. *Deceived by the Light*. Eugene, OR: Harvest House Publishers, 1995.

Habermas, Gary R. and Moreland, J. P. *Immortality: The Other Side of Death*. Nashville, TN: Thomas Nelson Publishers, 1992.

197

Henry, Carl F. H., ed. *Basic Christian Doctrines*. Grand Rapids, MI: Baker Book House, 1983.

Hoekema, Anthony A. *The Bible and the Future*. Grand Rapids, MI: William B. Eerdmans, 1984.

Hoyt, Herman A. *The End Times*. Chicago, IL: Moody Press, 1969.

Kubler-Ross, Elisabeth. *On Death and Dying*. New York: Macmillan Publishing Company, 1969.

Ladd, George Eldon. *The Last Things*. Grand Rapids, MI: William B. Eerdmans, 1982.

Milne, Bruce. *Know the Truth*. Downers Grove, IL: InterVarsity Press, 1982.

Moody, Raymond. *Life After Life*. New York: Bantam Books, 1976.

———. *Reflections on Life After Life*. New York: Bantam Books, 1978.

Morey, Robert A. *Death and the Afterlife*. Minneapolis, MN: Bethany House Publishers, 1984.

Pache, Rene. *The Future Life*. Chicago, IL: Moody Press, 1980.

Packer, J. I., ed. *Alive to God: Studies in Spirituality*. Downers Grove, IL: InterVarsity Press, 1992.

———. *Knowing God*. Downers Grove, IL: InterVarsity Press, 1973.

Pentecost, J. Dwight. *Things to Come*. Grand Rapids, MI: Zondervan Publishing House, 1974.

Rawlings, Maurice. *Beyond Death's Door*. New York: Bantam Books, 1979.

Rhodes, Ron. *Angels Among Us: Separating Truth from Fiction*. Eugene, OR: Harvest House Publishers, 1995.

Ring, Kenneth. *Life at Death: A Scientific Investigation of the Near-Death Experience*. New York: Coward, McCann, and Geoghegan, 1980.

Robinson, Haddon W. *Grief*. Grand Rapids, MI: Zondervan Publishing House, 1976.

Ryrie, Charles C. *A Survey of Bible Doctrine*. Chicago, IL: Moody Press, 1980.

———. *Basic Theology*. Wheaton, IL: Victor Books, 1986.

Sauer, Eric. *From Eternity to Eternity*. Grand Rapids, MI: William B. Eerdmans, 1979.

Smith, Wilbur M. *The Biblical Doctrine of Heaven*. Chicago, IL: Moody Press, 1974.

Taylor, Rick. *When Life Is Changed Forever.* Eugene, OR: Harvest House Publishers, 1992.

Thiessen, Henry Clarence. *Lectures in Systematic Theology.* Grand Rapids, MI: William B. Eerdmans, 1981.

Unger, Merrill F. *Beyond the Crystal Ball.* Chicago, IL: Moody Press, 1973.

Walvoord, John F., and Chafer, Lewis Sperry. *Major Bible Themes.* Grand Rapids, MI: Zondervan Publishing House, 1975.

Wesley, John. *The Nature of Salvation.* Minneapolis, MN: Bethany House Publishers, 1987.

Wright, Rusty. *The Other Side of Life.* San Bernardino, CA: Here's Life Publishers, 1979.

Zodhiates, Spiros. *Life After Death.* Chattanooga, TN: AMG Publishers, 1989.

Endnotes

Introduction: The Undiscovered Country

1. Electronic online version of "Hamlet." Produced by The Gutenberg Project. Downloaded from America Online.
2. Rene Pache, *The Future Life* (Chicago, IL: Moody Press, 1980). p. 211.
3. *More Gathered Gold*. Electronic Hypercard database version. Downloaded from The Servant BBS.
4. *Bible Illustrations for Preaching,* electronic media, Hypercard database, © 1991 by Michael Green.
5. David C. Needham, *Birthright: Christian, Do You Know Who You Are?* (Portland, OR: Multnomah Press, 1981), p. 12.

Chapter 1—Entering Death's Door

1. Edythe Draper, *Draper's Book of Quotations for the Christian World* (Wheaton, IL: Tyndale House Publishers, 1992), p. 127.
2. "Death," in *The 1995 Grolier Multimedia Encyclopedia* (electronic media), © 1994 by Grolier Electronic Publishing, Inc.
3. John Blanchard, *Whatever Happened to Hell?* (Durham, England: Evangelical Press, 1993), p. 47.
4. John Barry, "The Changing American Way of Death," *Orange County Register*, July 4, 1994, electronic online version.
5. "Death," in *The Concise Columbia Encyclopedia* (electronic media © 1994, licensed from Columbia University Press), in "Microsoft Bookshelf 94."
6. Blanchard, p. 67.
7. Blanchard, p. 59.
8. All the deathbed statements are found in Paul Lee Tan, *Encyclopedia of 7,700 Illustrations* (Rockville, MD: Assurance Publishers, 1985), p. 314.

Chapter 2—Life in the Intermediate State

1. Edythe Draper, *Draper's Book of Quotations for the Christian World* (Wheaton, IL: Tyndale House Publishers, 1992), p. 139.

2. Charles Spurgeon, "Death," in *Spurgeon Quotes*, electronic media, Hypercard database.

3. Billy Graham, *Angels: God's Secret Agents* (Garden City, NY: Doubleday & Co., 1975), p. 152.

4. Theologian Herman Hoyt, however, believes Christians will have an intermediate body in the intermediate state. He bases this on 2 Corinthians 5:1-4. *See* Herman Hoyt, *The End Times* (Chicago, IL: Moody Press, 1969), p. 46.

5. *Bible Illustrations for Preaching*, electronic media, Hypercard database, © 1991 by Michael Green.

6. Anthony A. Hoekema, *The Bible and the Future* (Grand Rapids, MI: William B. Eerdmans, 1984), p. 99.

7. Hoyt, p. 37.

8. Spiros Zodhiates, *Life After Death* (Chattanooga, TN: AMG Publishers, 1989), p. 71; Robert A. Morey, *Death and the Afterlife* (Minneapolis, MN: Bethany House Publishers, 1984), p. 86; Henry Clarence Thiessen, *Lectures in Systematic Theology* (Grand Rapids, MI: William B. Eerdmans, 1981), p. 381; Hoyt, p. 37.

9. Morey, p. 86.

10. Other scholars, however, do not believe Ephesians 4:8 refers to Christ leading captives out of Hades into heaven. *See* Zodhiates, p. 77; Charles C. Ryrie, *Basic Theology* (Wheaton, IL: Victor Books, 1986), p. 519.

11. There are also Bible scholars who deny the two-compartment theory of Hades. Theologian Charles Ryrie is one of these. He states that "Abraham's bosom is not said to be in Hades but rather 'far away' from it. Abraham's bosom is a figurative phrase for paradise, or the presence of God. It was paradise promised to the repentant thief by the Lord (Luke 23:43), not a blissful compartment of Hades."

Moreover, Ryrie asks, "Are we to understand that Elijah was taken at his translation to Sheol/Hades and not heaven? I think not; rather, the Old Testament saint went immediately to heaven to wait for the resurrection of his body at the second coming of Christ."

Whichever view is correct, they both agree that the intermediate state for believers is one of rest and peace, while the intermediate state for unbelievers is one of torment. *See* Ryrie, p. 520.

12. Douglas Connelly, *What the Bible Really Says: After Life* (Downers Grove, IL: InterVarsity Press, 1995), p. 18.

13. "Today in the Word," April 10, 1993. Cited in the World Wide Web page (Internet) of Dallas Theological Seminary, *Illustrations*, electronic media database.

14. Charles Spurgeon, "Death," in *Spurgeon Quotes*.

15. Morey, p. 86.

16. Hoekema, p. 102.

Chapter 3—Alive Forevermore: The Future Resurrection

1. Edythe Draper, *Draper's Book of Quotations for the Christian World* (Wheaton, IL: Tyndale House Publishers, 1992), p. 533.

2. George Eldon Ladd, *The Last Things* (Grand Rapids, MI: William B. Eerdmans, 1982), p. 37.

3. Canon Westcott, *The Gospel of the Resurrection*, cited in the World Wide Web page (Internet) of Dallas Theological Seminary, *Illustrations*, electronic media.

4. Sir Edward Clarke; cited by John Stott, *Basic Christianity* (Downers Grove, IL: InterVarsity Press, 1971), p. 47.

5. Cited by Wilbur Smith, *Sermons on the Christian Life*; cited in the World Wide Web page (Internet) of Dallas Theological Seminary, *Illustrations*, electronic media.

6. *The New International Dictionary of New Testament Theology*, ed. Colin Brown, vol. 2 (Grand Rapids, MI: Zondervan Publishing House, 1979), p. 45.

7. Walter C. Kaiser, *Hard Sayings of the Old Testament* (Downers Grove, IL: InterVarsity Press, 1988), p. 83.

8. Kaiser, p. 83.

9. Kaiser, p. 84.

10. Kaiser, p. 84.

11. Robert L. Reymond, *Jesus, Divine Messiah: The New Testament Witness* (Phillipsburg, NJ: Presbyterian and Reformed Publishing Co., 1990), p. 161.

12. Anthony A. Hoekema, *The Bible and the Future* (Grand Rapids, MI: William B. Eerdmans, 1984), p. 248.

13. John Calvin: cited in John Blanchard, *Whatever Happened to Hell?* (Durham, England: Evangelical Press, 1993), p. 97.

14. George Sweeting, *Great Quotes and Illustrations* (Waco, TX: Word Books, 1985), p. 217.

Chapter 4—Heaven: The Eternal City of God

1. Edythe Draper, *Draper's Book of Quotations for the Christian World* (Wheaton, IL: Tyndale House Publishers, 1992), p. 307.

2. Douglas Connelly, *What the Bible Really Says: After Life* (Downers Grove, IL: InterVarsity Press, 1995), p. 92.

3. Henry M. Morris, *The Biblical Basis for Modern Science* (Grand Rapids, MI: Baker Book House, 1984), p. 156.

4. Morris, p. 156.

5. John MacArthur, *The Superiority of Christ* (Chicago, IL: Moody Press, 1986), pp. 33-34.

6. Eric Sauer, *From Eternity to Eternity* (Grand Rapids, MI: Eerdmans, 1979), p. 30.

7. Millard Erickson, *Christian Theology* (Grand Rapids, MI: Baker Book House, 1987), p. 1229.

8. Cited in Tim LaHaye, *Revelation: Illustrated and Made Plain* (Grand Rapids, MI: Zondervan Publishing House, 1975), p. 315.

9. Merrill F. Unger, *Beyond the Crystal Ball* (Chicago, IL: Moody Press, 1973), p. 173.

10. Unger, p. 173.

11. John Gill, "Hebrews 11:13-15" in *The Online Bible* (electronic media), version 2.5.2.

12. Bruce Shelley, *Theology for Ordinary People* (Downers Grove, IL: InterVarsity Press, 1994), p. 212.

13. John F. Walvoord, *The Church in Prophecy* (Grand Rapids, MI: Zondervan Publishing House, 1964), p. 164.

14. Lewis Sperry Chafer, *Systematic Theology*, ed. John F. Walvoord (Wheaton, IL: Victor Books, 1989), p. 284.

Chapter 5—The Blessing of Heaven for Believers

1. Charles Spurgeon, "Spurgeon's Quotes," Hypercard stack, electronic media.

2. Bruce Milne, *Know the Truth* (Downers Grove, IL: InterVarsity Press, 1982), p. 278.

3. Douglas Connelly, *What the Bible Really Says: After Life* (Downers Grove, IL: InterVarsity Press, 1995), p. 101.

4. Anthony A. Hoekema, *The Bible and the Future* (Grand Rapids, MI: William B. Eerdmans, 1984), p. 280.

5. Merrill F. Unger, *Beyond the Crystal Ball* (Chicago, IL: Moody Press, 1973), p. 167.

6. Hoekema, p. 281.

7. Hoekema, p. 285.

Chapter 6—Heaven for Those Who Can't Believe

1. John B. Marchbanks, *Your Little One Is in Heaven* (Neptune, NJ: Loizeaux Brothers, 1951), p. 9.

2. G.N.M. Collins, "Infant Salvation," in *Evangelical Dictionary of Theology*, ed. Walter A. Elwell (Grand Rapids, MI: Baker Book House, 1984), p. 560.

3. Robert Lightner, *Heaven for Those Who Can't Believe* (Schaumburg, IL: Regular Baptist Press, 1977), p. 10; cf. Charles C. Ryrie, *Basic Theology* (Wheaton, IL: Victor Books, 1986), pp. 218-21; Louis Berkhof, *Manual of Christian Doctrine* (Grand Rapids, MI: Eerdmans, 1983), pp. 143-45; Henry Clarence Thiessen, *Lectures in Systematic Theology* (Grand Rapids, MI: Eerdmans, 1981), pp. 173-82.

4. Lightner, p. 10.

5. Millard J. Erickson, *Christian Theology* (Grand Rapids, MI: Baker Book House, 1985), p. 639.

6. Lightner, p. 18.

7. Lightner, pp. 19-25; cf. Ron Rhodes, *Christ Before the Manger: The Life and Times of the Preincarnate Christ* (Grand Rapids, MI: Baker Book House, 1992), pp. 43-48.

8. Lightner, p. 22.

9. J.I. Packer, *Knowing God* (Downers Grove, IL: InterVarsity Press, 1973), p. 138; cf. Lightner, p. 23.

10. *See* John Blanchard, *Whatever Happened to Hell?* (Durham, England: Evangelical Press, 1993), pp. 113-14.

11. Lightner, p. 33.

12. A question that comes up from time to time is, What about aborted or miscarried babies? Do they have eternal souls while they are yet in the womb? And do they go to heaven at the moment of death? I believe the answer to both questions is *yes*.

The Scriptures indicate that at the very moment of conception the babe in the womb possesses a soul. In this view, children receive from their parents—through conception—both their material part (the body) and immaterial part (the soul or spirit). Both body *and* soul are passed on from parents to children.

This view fits with the biblical evidence. For example, God's breathing into Adam the breath of life is not said to be repeated after Adam (Genesis 2:7). Moreover, Adam begat a son *in his own likeness*, and this would have to include Adam's *entire* likeness—both body *and* soul (Genesis 5:3).

Since babies in the womb have eternal souls, then all the arguments in this chapter regarding infant salvation apply to preborn infants as well. The moment a baby in the womb is aborted or miscarried, his or her soul or spirit departs from the body and goes directly to heaven.

Chapter 7—Hell: The Infernal Destiny of the Wicked

1. John Blanchard, *Whatever Happened to Hell?* (Durham, England: Evangelical Press, 1993), p. 13.

2. Blanchard, p. 15.

3. V. Cruz, "Gehenna," in *Evangelical Dictionary of Theology*, ed. Walter A. Elwell (Grand Rapids, MI: Baker Book House, 1984), p. 439.

4. Blanchard, p. 156.

5. Blanchard, p. 156.

6. Robert L. Thomas, "2 Thessalonians," *The Expositor's Bible Commentary*, ed. Frank E. Gaebelein (Grand Rapids, MI: Zondervan Publishing House, 1978), p. 313.

7. Robert A. Morey. *Death and the Afterlife* (Minneapolis, MN: Bethany House Publishers, 1984), p. 138.

8. Alan Gomes, "Evangelicals and the Annihilation of Hell," Part One, *Christian Research Journal*, Spring 1991, p. 17.

9. John Gerstner; cited in Gomes, p. 18.

10. Gomes, p. 18.

11. Alan Gomes, "Evangelicals and the Annihilation of Hell." Part Two, *Christian Research Journal*, Summer 1991, p. 11.

12. Shirley MacLaine, *Out on a Limb* (New York: Bantam Books, 1983), p. 233.

Chapter 8—The Judgment of Humankind

1. John Wesley, *The Nature of Salvation* (Minneapolis, MN: Bethany House Publishers, 1987), p. 134.

2. J.I. Packer, *Knowing God* (Downers Grove, IL: InterVarsity Press, 1983), p. 126.

3. John Blanchard, *Whatever Happened to Hell?* (Durham, England: Evangelical Press, 1993), p. 113.

4. Douglas Connelly, *What the Bible Really Says: After Life* (Downers Grove, IL: InterVarsity Press, 1995), p. 119.

5. Cited in Charles C. Ryrie, *Basic Theology* (Wheaton, IL: Victor Books, 1986), p. 513.

6. Connelly, p. 118.

7. Merrill F. Unger, *Beyond the Crystal Ball* (Chicago, IL: Moody Press, 1973), p. 63.

8. Wesley, p. 135.

9. Wesley, p. 135.

10. Blanchard, p. 116.

11. J. Dwight Pentecost, *Things to Come* (Grand Rapids, MI: Zondervan Publishing House, 1974), p. 226.

12. Lewis Sperry Chafer and John F. Walvoord, *Major Bible Themes* (Grand Rapids, MI: Zondervan Publishing House, 1975), p. 343.

13. Wesley, p. 130.

Chapter 9—Near-Death Experiences

1. Kenneth Ring, *Life at Death: A Scientific Investigation of the Near-Death Experience* (New York: Coward, McCann, and Geoghegan, 1980), p. 22.

2. Jerry Yamamoto, "The Near-Death Experience," *Christian Research Journal*, Spring 1992, p. 6.

3. Rusty Wright, *The Other Side of Life* (San Bernardino, CA: Here's Life Publishers. 1979), p. 1.

4. Yamamoto. p. 2.

5. Yamamoto, p. 2.

6. Quoted in John Ankerberg and John Weldon, *The Facts on Life After Death* (Eugene, OR: Harvest House Publishers, 1992), p. 19.

7. Ankerberg and Weldon, p. 7.

8. Doug Groothuis, *Deceived by the Light* (Eugene, OR: Harvest House Publishers, 1995), p. 11.

9. Betty J. Eadie with Curtis Taylor, *Embraced by the Light* (Placerville, CA: Gold Leaf Press, 1992), pp. 40-42; cited in Groothuis, p. 13.

10. Groothuis, p. 20.

11. Groothuis, p. 22.

12. Eadie, p. 28.

13. Eadie; cited in Groothuis, p. 24.

14. Eadie, p. 113.

15. Eadie, p. 94.

16. Eadie, p. 71.

17. Eadie, p. 85.

18. Eadie, p. 81.

19. Groothuis, p. 39.

20. Charles Garfield; cited in Ankerberg and Weldon, p. 28.

21. Doug Groothuis, pp. 70-71.

22. Ankerberg and Weldon, p. 8.

23. Ankerberg and Weldon, p. 10.

24. Ankerberg and Weldon, p. 11.

25. Kenneth Ring; cited in Ankerberg and Weldon, p. 21.

26. Rodney Clapp, "Rumors of Heaven," *Christianity Today*, October 7, 1988, p. 20.

27. Douglas Connelly, *What the Bible Really Says: After Life* (Downers Grove, IL: InterVarsity Press, 1995), p. 35.

28. Kenneth Ring; cited in Ankerberg and Weldon, p. 3.

29. Yamamoto, p. 5.

30. Yamamoto, p. 5.

31. Yamamoto, p. 5.

32. Gary R. Habermas and J.P. Moreland, *Immortality: The Other Side of Death* (Nashville, TN: Thomas Nelson Publishers, 1992), p. 93.

Chapter 10—Helping Those Who Grieve

1. Edythe Draper, *Draper's Book of Quotations for the Christian World* (Wheaton, IL: Tyndale House Publishers, 1992), p. 289.

2. "Grief," in *Illustrations*, World Wide Web page (Internet) of Dallas Theological Seminary, electronic media.

3. Rick Taylor, *When Life Is Changed Forever* (Eugene, OR: Harvest House Publishers, 1992), p. 120.

4. Taylor, p. 120.

5. C.S. Lewis, *A Grief Observed*; cited in Taylor, p. 50.

6. Sharan Morris, *Grief and How to Live with It*, p. 18; cited in Haddon W. Robinson, *Grief* (Grand Rapids, MI: Zondervan Publishing House, 1976), p. 9.

7. *Home Living* magazine, May 1980. In *Illustrations*, World Wide Web page (Internet) of Dallas Theological Seminary, electronic media.

Chapter 11—Looking Toward Eternity

1. Edythe Draper, *Draper's Book of Quotations for the Christian World* (Wheaton, IL: Tyndale House Publishers, 1992), p. 180.

2. J.I. Packer, ed. *Alive to God: Studies in Spirituality* (Downers Grove, IL: InterVarsity Press, 1992), p. 162.

3. Packer, p. 171.

4. Packer, p. 171.

5. Packer, p. 163.

6. Packer, p. 164.

7. Packer, p. 165.

8. Packer, p. 165.

9. Richard Baxter; cited in Packer, p. 167.

10. Gary R. Habermas and J.P. Moreland, *Immortality: The Other Side of Death* (Nashville, TN: Thomas Nelson Publishers, 1992), p. 185.

11. Habermas and Moreland, p. 186.

12. John Calvin, *Institutes of the Christian Religion*, ed. John T. McNeill (Philadelphia: The Westminster Press, n.d.), p. 590.

13. John Wesley, *The Nature of Spiritual Growth* (Minneapolis, MN: Bethany House Publishers, 1987), p. 189.

14. Charles Spurgeon; cited by Jim Elliot, *Shadow of the Almighty* (Grand Rapids, MI: Zondervan Publishing House, 1970), p. 83.

15. "Fear of Death," World Wide Web page (Internet) of Dallas Theological Seminary, *Illustrations*, electronic media.

Postscript: An Invitation to Believe

1. Edythe Draper, *Draper's Book of Quotations for the Christian World* (Wheaton, IL: Tyndale House Publishers, 1992), p. 539.

Appendix: What About Suicide?

1. *See* Charles Ryrie, *You Mean the Bible Teaches That?* (Chicago: Moody Press, 1978), p. 78.